W0007569

Portuguese

How to Learn Portuguese Fast, Including Grammar, Short Stories, and Useful Phrases

Contents

Introduction

Knowing more than one language is essential in many working environments. Globalization has made the world smaller, and thus, connecting to other people, sharing information and knowledge, while working together towards the same goal, has become inevitable. However, to do so successfully, the language barrier has to be overcome. Moreover, while it is true that English is the language more widely spoken across the globe, many other idioms are in high demand, and that may be very valuable in the near future, either for your personal or professional life. Portuguese is, without a doubt, one of them. Being the sixth most spoken language in the world, and the official language of Portugal, Brazil, Angola, Cape Verde, São Tomé and Príncipe, Guinea Bissau, Mozambique, Equatorial Guinea, and East Timor, Portuguese is, now more than ever, a skill very much worth having. This book aims to do just that—teach you the essentials of this new skill. At the very least, it is expected that *Portuguese: How to Learn Portuguese Fast, Including Grammar, Short Stories, and Useful Phrases* sets out the fundamentals of the language, allowing you to have the tools you need to carry on this path of knowledge.

When learning a language, you are learning so much more than a few words and grammar rules. You are subtly getting an insight into the thinking process involved in the creation of the language, the vast culture that encompasses a country, or several, the differences in customs and traditions, the expressions, and how they came about, and so much more. As you progress, you will find that the Portuguese language is complex and rich—just like its history and culture. So, if you feel discouraged at any point, think about how you're not only mastering a new skill, which takes time, but also, and more importantly, that you're getting to know a part of the world's history while enabling yourself to connect with others. How, you might ask? Because the role of the knowledge of a language is pivotal, as it allows people to bond with one another. It allows us to reach out, to share personal experiences and feelings, and to understand and be understood. Moreover, in a world in which everyone is struggling to acknowledge, accept and tolerate others, it is important that we start using language and words as the first and ultimate weapon. It is the supreme tool that enables every one of us to have a voice, be heard, and, much more importantly, to hear, listen, and understand—and, consequently, to empathize and connect. Besides, did you know that Portuguese derives from Latin? Because of that, Portuguese can be a great starting point to learn other Romance languages like French, Italian or Spanish. They share numerous words while many others are very similar; something you will definitely notice as soon as your vocabulary becomes richer.

So, the only thing left to do is wish you… ***Boa sorte!***

A Few Tips about Portuguese

The Portuguese Language has evolved throughout the years to adapt to its organic changes, current ways of speaking it and also to unite and unify it throughout the different Portuguese speaking countries. The Orthographic Agreement of 1990 has changed the spelling of many words and made the written PT Portuguese much more similar to the spoken BR Portuguese. Even though the agreement is from 1990, it was only applied in Portugal in 2010. However, there is some controversy when it comes to the use of this agreement; thus, many authors, writers, journalists, and academics choose to write in agreement with the Portuguese prior to the 1990 Orthographic Agreement. That is also the choice made in this book. However, if we think there might be something you need to be aware of, we will let you know. Nevertheless, if after reading this book, you read a Portuguese book or newspaper in which some words are spelled slightly different from what you have learned, don't worry. Both versions are equally accepted socially.

So, you already know that Portuguese is spoken in many countries around the world. The language is fundamentally the same throughout those countries, but it is only natural that some words, the pronunciation, the accents, popular sayings, and things of this nature, differ. A Portuguese-speaking person will undoubtedly understand another, regardless of where they come from. Nevertheless, all countries have throughout their extension many different accents, obviously. Some of them may even be really hard to understand for natives, so don't get frustrated if you happen to meet a Portuguese-speaking native with a thick accent—just ask him or her to speak slower or to *falar mais devagar, por favor!* Granted, that for the ones who are just beginning to learn the language, it can be confusing and even counter-productive to be presented to multiple countries' Portuguese at the same time. With that in mind, the choice of this book was to follow the Portuguese from Portugal norms. That includes sayings, pronunciation, spelling, and wording. However, because Brazil is becoming a very important country in the political scene, besides being a very popular tourist destination, some of the differences between both languages will be approached and presented to the reader, so that it is easier to make the transition and adapt. Again, whichever "version" of Portuguese you speak will be understood worldwide, but it is better to be acquainted with specific Brazilian terms so that everything goes smoothly if you ever happen to visit Brazil or meet a Brazilian. The differences can be compared to US English and British English, so there's not much to worry about.

One thing, however, that is worthy of being mentioned is the very Portuguese practice of being formal, linguistically, to show respect. Whenever a person is talking to someone they don't know, or just don't know very well, someone older, someone higher up in a hierarchical position, or even in a work environment, with coworkers, instead of the "tu" = "you" being used, the word "você" = "you" is used. But it isn't quite that simple. Even though using "tu" might not be appropriate, actually using or saying the word "você" isn't either. It may seem confusing, but when you're approaching someone and have to talk formally, you just omit the word "você", and continue building the sentence as if it was there all along. Then, instead of the verb being in the first person singular, the verb is conjugated in the third person singular, but «você» is either omitted or replaced by the person's name or just «o senhor / a senhora» (sir / ma'am). Look at these examples:

- Did you deliver the documents, sir? – *(Você) Entregou os documentos?* or *O senhor entregou os documentos?*
- You're doing a great job, ma'am! – *(Você) Está a fazer um trabalho fantástico!* or *A senhora está a fazer um trabalho fantástico!*
- Do you want to come by for dinner? – *(Você) Quer vir cá jantar?*

If this was an informal conversation, it would go like this:

- Did you deliver the documents? – *Tu entregaste os documentos?* or *Entregaste os documentos?*
- You're doing a great job! – *Tu estás a fazer um trabalho fantástico!* or *Estás a fazer um trabalho fantástico!*
- Do you want to come by for dinner? – *Tu queres vir cá jantar?* or *Queres vir cá jantar?*

With Brazilians, however, in the informal speech, instead of the word "tu", the word "você" is used. The sentences would be constructed as the first set of examples given, but without the omitted "você", meaning "você" is actually said. In the formal speech, there is a tendency to use "o senhor/a senhora" = "sir/madam" and hiding the "você". It may be hard to perceive or identify these differences and knowing how to use what and when. But there is no reason to fret. Learning a language as rich and complex as Portuguese takes time and effort. And it is that same effort that will be taken into account by the Portuguese. They will love the fact that you're speaking their language and may even help you with some tips.

Regarding the organization of the book, it starts by presenting the alphabet and how to pronounce each letter. Moving on, you will find how a sentence is built in Portuguese—we will start by deconstructing it to then, hopefully, enable you to build it from scratch. We'll approach several elements of the Portuguese grammar, namely the ones we deem absolutely fundamental, and after that, you will find four short stories that will portray real-life situations, which will hopefully allow you to connect more organically to the Portuguese language by dealing with it in a more dynamic context. After the short stories, there is a chapter that contains varied basic sentences that you may use in case you're visiting any Portuguese speaking country. Right at the end of the book, you will find a few lists that may help you on several different occasions or in certain situations.

Throughout the book, there will also be some exercises to put your Portuguese abilities to the test. After each short story—which is translated into English to facilitate comprehension—there will be a small quiz to test a wide variety of subjects. Every quiz, test or question is solved, but try to complete everything without looking for the right answer. Equally important is to follow the order of the book, and to read everything through and through (except for the pocket dictionary—go there any time you need, especially in the beginning), not just bits, at least in the first reading or first couple of readings. An overall view or understanding will make everything sink in more easily, even if, at first, it seems to be somewhat confusing.

Lastly, a few final tips to help you:
- Speak to yourself in Portuguese whenever you can;
- Walk around the house naming objects in Portuguese;
- Connect words to images. The memory clues images trigger will definitely help you retain the knowledge of what you have been studying;
- Try to think in Portuguese;
- If you know someone who's also trying to learn Portuguese, talk and write to them always in Portuguese and correct each other.

And now, we're all set. Let's start!

Chapter 1 – First Things First

Alphabet

Vowels

When saying the vowels a, e, i, o, u, they should sound like this: "a", like the "a" in "car; the "e", like the "e" in "tell"; "i", like the "ee" in "seed"; "o", like the "o" in "door"; and finally "u", like the "u" in "super". However, as we have seen many times throughout this book, things are not quite so simple. At several other times, for several other words, the way you read these vowels will depend on the words and the combination of letters. In fact, the sound the vowels "a", "e" and "o" make vary a lot since they have four different types of pronunciation:

    a) Open pronunciation;
    b) Closed pronunciation;
    c) Reduced pronunciation;
    d) Nasal pronunciation.

Below you'll find how every vowel is pronounced in each different situation.

    ➢ **"a":**

a) Like the "a" in "cat". This sound sometimes happens in the stressed syllable of a word, or if it contains the diacritical mark " ′ ";

b) Used when the "a" is at the end of the word but can be in the stressed syllable or anywhere else in the word. It is the case of the first two letters "a" on the name "Mariana". It sounds similar to the "u" in "butter";

c) This happens when the "a" is at the end of a word. The sound is reduced or almost non-existent. Again, with the name "Mariana", the pronunciation, if written, would look something like "ma-rian", the last "a" being practically non-existent;

d) In the word "ananás", the first two vowels are followed by a nasal sound, which makes them sound like the "a" in "anthropologist". With the diacritical marks "^" or "~", this vowel will also sound nasal.

➤ **"e":**

a) Like the "e" in "pet", when it is in the accentuated syllable or if it has the acute accent " ′ ";

b) When an "e" is not at the end of the word but can be in the stressed syllable. The sound is something similar to the "a" in "answer";

c) When the "e" is at the end of the word or between two consonants in the non-stressed syllable. The sound is very reduced or almost non-existent;

d) It will sound like the "e" in "enthusiasm". The diacritical mark "^" will also make it sound nasal.

➤ **"i" and "u":**

These two vowels are pronounced only with an open pronunciation. In a few words, they can also sound reduced when they are in between two consonants in a non-stressed syllable.

➤ **"o":**

a) When it is in the accentuated syllable or if it contains an acute accent;

b) When the "o" is not at the end of the word but can be in the stressed syllable. The sound is something similar to the "ou" sound in "soul";

c) When the "o" is at the end of the word, in a non-stressed syllable, or just by itself, as a definite article. This makes the "o" sound like an "u" or "oo", like in the word "super";

d) Like in the case of "a" and "e", this type of pronunciation happens every time the vowel is followed by an "n" or "m" or contains the diacritical mark "^" or "~". In words like "ponte" (bridge), the vowel will come out pretty nasalized, and it will sound something like "on" in the word "among".

Consonants

➤ **"B"** – always sounds just like the "b" in the word base;

➤ **"C"** – when it is followed by either an "e" or an "i", it has a soft sound as in "center". Followed by either an "a", "o", or "u", it has a hard sound as in "car".

➤ **"D"** – sounds as it does in English;

➤ **"F"** – sounds as it does in English;

➤ **"G"** – when is followed by an "a", "o", or "u", it has a hard sound like the "g" in "gun". When it is followed by an "e" or "I", it sounds like the "s" in "leisure";

➤ **"H"** – always silent in Portuguese, as it is in the word "hour";

➤ **"J"** – always pronounced like the "s" in leisure, no matter which vowel follows it;

➤ **"L"** – at the beginning of a word and between vowels, it always sounds like the "l" in "late". At the end of the word, it sounds just like it does in English;

➤ **"M"** – at the beginning of a word and between vowels, it sounds like the "m" in the word "mom". At the end of a word, it has a sound similar to the "n" in the word "cent";

➤ **"N"** – makes the same sound as the English "n" does, before or between vowels;

- ➤ **"P"** – sounds the same as in English;
- ➤ **"Q"** – sounds the same as "k";
- ➤ **"R"** – at the beginning of a word and when doubled, it has a hard sound, which is not very common in English. It can be somewhat similar to a hard accent when saying the words "hell" or "hot". When at the end of a word, or before or after a vowel, it has a soft sound, as the "r" in "heart";

- ➤ **"S"** – has a soft sound as in "salt" when it is positioned at the beginning of a word no matter which vowel follows it, and also when it's doubled. Before a consonant, it sounds hard as the "sh" in the word "shoe". Between two vowels, it sounds like a "z";
- ➤ **"T"** – sounds the same as in English;
- ➤ **"V"** – sounds the same as in English;
- ➤ **"X"** – the letter "x" can make several sounds – "s", "ch", "z", "cs", and "ss". The most usual sound is the "ch" sound, which is always used when "x" is at the beginning of a word, and it sounds like the "sh" in the word "shoe". At the end of a word, it always sounds as "cs", like "x" in the word "next".
- ➤ **"Z"** – sounds the same as in English. However, when it is at the end of a word, it sounds like "sh", as in "shot".

Pronunciation

The pronunciation of the words is probably one of the hardest things to get right when learning a language. If you study enough, you will master the mechanics of a language—its grammar and vocabulary—but getting the accent and the correct pronunciation right is almost always a hassle. Some people have it naturally—a gift that makes them have an aptitude for pronouncing words in other languages just like natives. In the end, it doesn't matter if the pronunciation is native-like—if you're understood and pronounce words correctly, you're all set. However, to achieve that (and especially if you want to have that native accent), you have to understand how to pronounce every word, and what rule applies to each word, depending on digraphs, diphthongs, or diacritical marks particularities.

To make things harder, it's possible to create new sounds in Portuguese by combining two letters in pairs like "ss", "rr", "lh", "nh", and "ch"; when using accent signs over the vowels (á, é, ó, ú, ê, ô, ã, õ, à); and when using the cedilla under the c – "ç". Here is what you should do to more easily identify where the stress syllable is, so you know where to accentuate the tone.

➤ **Check the word to see if there is an accent:**

If you find a tilde (~), an acute accent (´), a grave stress (`) or a circumflex mark (^), the stress will be on that syllable. So, if you have the word "ananás" (pineapple), and you divide the word into syllables, "A-na-nás", the stress will fall on the last syllable because that is where the diacritical mark is. Therefore, we have the following pronunciation: "a-na-*nás*", the highlighted letters being the stress syllables.

- Co-ra-*ção* (heart);
- *Fá*-cil (easy);
- *Grá*-tis (free);
- Con-fu-*são* (confusion);
- So-*má*-li-a (somalia).

So, remember: the first thing you should do is to check for a stress mark like the ones described, and if the word has one of those, then it will be easy to know where the stress of the word should go and which syllable you should pronounce more.

➤ **When the word does not have a diacritical mark, then the stress of the word generally goes into the penultimate (i.e., the one before the last) syllable:**

This is the second most important rule because, in general, words that are not accentuated by a stress mark have their penultimate syllable accentuated instead. For instance, the word "caminho" (path/way), which is divided into three syllables, "ca-mi-nho", has its stress syllable in "mi". As you can see, the penultimate syllable is the one stressed since no diacritical mark tells us otherwise.

Check out some other examples:

- Co-*mi*-da (Food);
- A-ven-tu-*rei*-ro (Adventurous);
- Ca-sa-*men*-to (Marriage);
- Com-pa-*nhi*-a (Company).

From the examples above you can conclude that the length of the word is not important. Whether it has two, three, four or even more syllables, if it does not have a diacritical mark, it will generally have its stress in the penultimate syllable.

Nevertheless, and even though this rule is applied in most of the cases, there are, of course, some exceptions. Here are some of those:

➤ **Word ending in "i", "l", "r", "z", "im", "um", "ins", "uns":**

In those cases, instead of being in the penultimate syllable, the stress shifts to the final syllable:

- Pa-*pel* (paper);
- Co-*mer* (eat);
- Sen-*ti* (I felt);
- A-*tum* (tuna);
- Vo-*raz* (voracious);
- Pin-gu-*im* (penguin);
- Pin-gu-*ins* (penguins);
- Al-*guns* (some).

➤ **The sound of "lh" pair:**

When an "l" is paired with an "h", the sound of the "lh" pair is somewhat similar to the double "l" in the word "million". However, you need to make sure the tip of your tongue touches the internal part of the top of your front teeth as you're pronouncing the syllable that contains the "lh" pair.

➢ The sound of "nh" pair:

When an "n" is paired with an "nh", the sound of the "nh" pair is the same sound as that of the "ñ" in Spanish. Unfortunately, there is no equivalent in the English language from which we can draw comparisons.

➢ The sound of "ch" pair:

When a "c" is paired with a "ch", you get the pair "ch", which sounds the same way as the "sh" sound in English, just like in the word "she".

➢ The sound of vowels with accent marks:

In Portuguese, the sound of the vowels changes when accent marks are used. Four different kinds of accent marks can be used on top of the vowels: acute (á, é, í, ó, ú), circumflex (ê, ô), tilde (ã, õ), and grave accent (à).

- The acute accent makes the vowels have an open sound:
  - Já, like the "a" in the word "bar";
  - Raíz, like the pronunciation of the letter "e" in English;
  - Café, like the letter "e" in the word "bed";
  - Avó, like the word "oh";
  - Baú, like the second "u" in the word "kung-fu".
- The circumflex makes the vowels sound closed:
  - Você, like the sound of the beginning of the word "hence";
  - Avô, like the beginning of the word "oat".
- The tilde makes the vowels sound nasal:
  - Mão;
  - Limões;
  - Capitães.
- The grave accent is used to indicate the contraction of two words represented by one word in a sentence, rather than for creating a new sound; for instance, the feminine definite

article "a" (the) and the preposition "a" (to). They become one word, and the grave accent is used on it, so "a" + "a" = "à". In this case, the sound of the "a" does not change at all. It continues the same as the name of the letter "a" in the alphabet, as well as the "á" (with the acute accent), as mentioned above.

> ### The sound of the "ç":

When the cedilla is used under a "c", the hard sound before an "a" or an "o" changes to the soft sound, like the "s" in the word "some".

> ### The sound of nasal diphthongs:

A nasal sound is a sound you produce forcing the air out of your nose. That is what happens, or what should happen when you pronounce the letters "m" and "n" in Portuguese. If the word ends in a diphthong—two vowels that are read together to form a single sound—like "ão", "au", "ao", "õe", "oi", "ãe", "ai", "ou", "ei", "ui", the stress also shifts to the end. For instance, if you have a word like "Macau", the stress will be in the last syllable, because this word ends with a diphthong.

Singular and plural

In Portuguese, nouns and adjectives both have plural forms. So, the first thing to retain is that in Portuguese, an adjective, in relation to the noun, has to agree in gender—masculine or feminine—and in number—singular or plural. We will find out more about the gender of words later. For now, let's focus on the singular or plural.

> ### Words ending in a vowel:

As a general rule, with words that end with a vowel, all you need to add is an "s" at the end. However, it can't be that easy, can it? Obviously, there are some exceptions. You should, in this sense, make sure when you're applying the rule that you're not coming across an exception. We will check out some situations in which words ending in a vowel don't follow this rule soon. Here are some examples of the general rule being applied:

- Cama leve (light bed) = camas leves
- Menina bonita (pretty girl) = meninas bonitas
- Menino alto (tall boy) = meninos altos

➤ **Words ending in an "l":**

With words that end in either "al" or "ul", just cut the "l" off and add an "is" to the end of it. If the word ends in either an "el" or "ol", cut the "l" off and add an "is" to the word, just like the previous case, but also add an acute accent " ´ " to those vowels "e" and "o". If the word ends in "il", just add an "s" to the word because the "i" is already there.

- Canal (canal) = canais
- Azul (blue) = azuis
- Anel (ring) = anéis
- Lençol (sheet) = lençóis
- Canil (dog pound) = canis

➤ **Words ending in "em":**

With words that end in "em", you take off the "m" and add "ns". If a word has an acute accent on the "é", you carry the accent to the plural form. For instance:

- Garagem (garage) = garagens
- Refém (hostage) = reféns

➤ **Words ending in "r", "s" or "z":**

With words that end in either "r", "s", or "z", you just add an "es" to the end of the word. Like so:

- Motor (motor) = motores
- Luz (light) = luzes

- Português (portuguese) = portugueses[1]
- Mês (month) = meses

> ### Words ending in "ão":

With words that end in "ão", there can be three different possibilities to form the plural. These are the options: "ões", "ães", and "ãos". There is no rule that you can follow every time. What is more usual is the "ões", but the only way for you to know which one to use is to memorize them. Don't worry about that—you'll get there with practice. Here are some examples:

- Leão (lion) = leões
- Coração (heart) = corações
- Capitão (captain) = capitães
- Pão (bread) = pães
- Mão (hand) = mãos
- Orgão (organ) = orgãos

Once again, several rules can help when trying to turn a singular into a plural. However, and as you know by now, rules don't always apply. So you really need to watch out for some odd cases and try to memorize them. Below, you'll find a list of some exceptions to the rules previously mentioned, to which you can come back to whenever you need to make sure what is the correct way to write a word—either in its plural or singular form.

For instance, just like in English, some words are always used in the plural form (the article that precedes the noun is also in its plural form):

- Glasses – (os) Óculos
- Pants – (as) Calças
- Sneakers – (os) Ténis

---

[1] Tip: whenever you come across a word ending in "s", in which the letter immediately before the "s" has a diacritical mark, you just need to add the "es" and take out the diacritical mark to use it in its plural form, as shown in the examples above.

Then there are words in Portuguese that are only used in their plural form, but they don't correspond to their translation in English:

- (ir de) Férias – (going on) Vacation
- (as) Costas – Back (body part)

Some words that end in "s" don't have a plural form, so they don't change when you're referring to more than one of that. For instance:

- 1 lápis (1 pencil) = 2 lápis
- 1 vírus (1 virus) = 2 vírus
- 1 atlas (1 atlas) = 2 atlas

Exercise

1) <u>Let's test what you just learned. Write down the plural form of the following words:</u>

a) Sabor

b) Sabonete

c) Grão

d) Cão

e) Carrocel

f) Anzol

g) Sul

h) Paisagem

i) Limão

j) País

k) Armazém

l) Juvenil

m) Mãe

n) Pires

o) Céu

p) Sobral

q) Giz

Answers

1) <u>Plural:</u>

a) Sabores

b) Sabonetes
c) Grãos
d) Cães
e) Carrocéis
f) Anzóis
g) Suis
h) Paisagens
i) Limões
j) Países
k) Armazéns
l) Juvenis
m) Mães
n) Pires
o) Céus
p) Sobrais
q) Gizes

Gender in Portuguese

As we stated before, words in Portuguese have a gender. That applies to nouns, adjectives, and definite and indefinite articles. In this chapter, we will go more in depth about the nouns' genders. Below, in the Adjectives chapter, we will also see some examples of how gender affects them. For now, we will focus on nouns. Let's see what this is all about.

➢ **Masculine and feminine nouns:**

Nouns are words which are used to label objects, animals or people. In Portuguese, there is no neutral gender—a noun will always be either feminine or masculine. There is one general rule that will help you identify the gender of the word the great majority of the time. Masculine words tend to end with an "o", whereas feminine nouns tend to end in an "a". The article that precedes the noun will also be of great help since it follows this rule. For instance:

- A faca – the knife

- O saco – the bag

However, some nouns don't follow the rule. Some nouns end in an "a" but are masculine. For example:

- O chá – the tea
- O gorila – the gorilla

> ### Nouns ending in an "e":

Many nouns ending in an "e" are masculine in gender. Take a look at this example:

- O café – the coffee
- O telefone – the telephone

However, some of them may have a feminine correspondent. That happens when the noun refers to a person or an animal, which obviously can be either masculine or feminine. The gender of a noun can be easily modified by simply changing the definite article that precedes the noun. The word is actually spelled the same way for both genders, but the article before it determines if it's masculine or feminine.

- O estudante – the male student
- A estudante – the female student
- A (mulher) árabe – the female arabian
- O (homem) árabe – the male arabian

There are obviously some exceptions. There are words which end in "e" that are only feminine. Take a look at some of those:

- A estante – the bookcase
- A corrente – the current
- A lebre – the hare
- ### Nouns ending in "ão":

Most nouns ending in "ão" are masculine, but some feminine nouns end in "ão" as well:

- O ladrão – the thief
- O limão – the lemon

- O pão – the bread
- O coração – the heart
- A canção – the song
- A mão – the hand

■ <u>Nouns ending in "em":</u>

Nouns ending in "em" can be either masculine or feminine but tend to be more feminine. Don't forget that nouns that refer to people are spelled the same way for both genders, and it's the article that precedes it that will distinguish which gender they are:

- O jovem – the young man
- A jovem – the young woman
- O refém – the male hostage
- A refém – the female hostage
- A mensagem – the message
- A miragem – the mirage

■ <u>Nouns ending in "or":</u>

As for the nouns ending in "or", they can also be either masculine or feminine:

- O calor – the heat
- O cantor – the singer
- O louvor – the praise
- A flor – the flower
- A dor – the pain

■ <u>Nouns ending in "iz"</u>

Once again, nouns ending in "iz" can either be masculine or feminine:

- O nariz – the nose

- A raiz – the root
- O verniz (das unhas) – (nail) varnish
- A imperatriz – the empress

- **Nouns ending in "el" and "eu":**

In this situation, there are no doubts—every noun that ends in either "el" or "eu" is masculine. Take a look at a few examples:

- O anel – the ring
- O mel – the honey
- O papel – the paper
- O céu – the sky/heaven
- O chapéu – the hat
- O réu – the defendant
- O véu – the veil

Exercise

1) Write down the feminine of each noun:

a) Conde

b) Patrão

c) Herói

d) Ladrão

e) Ateu

f) Actor

2) Choose the option in which every noun is masculine:

a) Profeta, assombração, fantasma;

b) Profeta, telefonema, fantasma;

c) Eclipse, alface, champanhe;

d) Assombração, mascote, grama;

3) Write down which nouns are feminine and which ones are masculine:

a) Tigresa ( )

b) Marido ( )

c) Poeta ( )

d) Irmã ( )

e) Teia ( )

f) Ré ( )

4) Rewrite the sentence in the masculine form:

a) A minha afilhada foi testemunha de um caso.

b) A ré apresentou-se no tribunal.

c) A judia chegou cedo ao encontro.

d) A baronesa falou com a rainha.

Answers

1) a) condessa; b) patroa; c) heroína; d) ladra; e) ateia f) actriz.

2) The correct answer is b).

3) a) F; b) M; c) M; d) F; e) F; f) F

4) a) O meu afilhado foi testemunha de um caso.

b) O réu apresentou-se no tribunal.

c) O judeu chegou cedo ao encontro.

d) O barão falou com o rei.

Capitalization

There are some differences between the English and the Portuguese language when it comes to the capitalization, or not, of some words. To make it clearer for you, we are going to write down the most important situations in which lowercase should be used, and the most important situations in which uppercase is the rule.

You should use lowercase when referring to:

- Common use of everyday vocabulary;
- Days of the week, months, seasons[2];
- Cardinal points, but not when they are abbreviated[3];

You should use uppercase when referring to:

- People's names;
- Cities, Countries;
- First word of a sentence;
- In nouns that refer to institutes or associations;
- Holidays and festive activities;
- Book titles;
- Acronyms.

Exercise

1) <u>**Let's test what you just learned. Which of the following should start with a capital letter?**</u>

    a) pedro
    b) sul
    c) sudoeste
    d) verão
    e) grã-bretanha
    f) mesa
    g) grão
    h) itália
    i) se (sudeste)
    j) terça-feira

---

[2] This is the rule after the 1990 Orthographic Agreement. As stated before, we are following the rules prior to the Agreement (and as you'll see, whenever any of these words come up throughout the book, they will be written in uppercase), but we thought it was important to make you aware of this.
[3] The same as with the days of the week, months, and seasons—before the New Orthographic Agreement, these words were written in uppercase.

k) dezembro
l) lisboa
m) inverno
n) peta (the animals association)
o) domingo
p) natal

1) The correct answers are a); e); h); i); l); n); p).

Chapter 2 – The Fundamentals

Grammar rules

Word order

You may have noticed by now that the word order in the Portuguese language is different from the word order in English. And that's true in several situations. You may also have realized that whereas in English you say, "Maria has a beautiful car", a Portuguese native speaker would, literally translated, instead say that "Maria has a car beautiful". The good news is that generally speaking, the structure of a sentence in Portuguese is not much different from the one in English. You only have to pay attention to specific cases. The Portuguese word order is **Subject > Verb > Object.** Let's see how that works in different phrase formations.

➢ In a statement:

If your sentence is a statement, you are expressing a fact. Normally, you are talking about a specific event. Let's analyze the following sentences in pairs—first the Portuguese and then the English ones, sentence by sentence. Please compare and contrast the Portuguese word order and the English one carefully.

Subject (s) > Verb (v) > Object (o) > Phrase Complement (pc)

- He has a house in Rio de Janeiro. – Ele (s) tem (v) uma casa (o) no Rio de Janeiro (pc).
- She washed her clothes in the washing machine. – Ela (s) lavou (v) a roupa (o) na máquina de lavar (pc).
- We read a book at the beach. – Nós (s) lemos (v) um livro (o) na praia (pc).
- They have salmon for lunch. – Eles (s) comem (v) salmão (o) ao almoço (pc).
- You sirs are going to schedule the meeting for tomorrow. – Os senhores (s) vão marcar (v) a reunião (o) para amanhã (pc).

Please be aware that when speaking in Portuguese, the subject is often hidden. This is something that was talked about in the "A Few Tips about Portuguese" chapter. What this means is that the verb itself indicates the subject of that sentence. For instance, instead of "Nós vamos à escola amanhã" (We are going to school tomorrow), it can simply be "*Vamos* à escola amanhã."

➤ In a description:

The descriptive word, or in other words, the adjective, usually needs to be placed after the noun. Let's see what this is all about with some examples:

Subject > Adjective 1 > Verb > Adjective 2

- The big house is beautiful. – A casa (s) grande (a1) é (v) bonita (a2).
- The ripe bananas are cheaper. – As bananas (s) maduras (a1) são (v) mais baratas (a2).
- An old car isn't expensive. – Um carro (s) velho (a1) não é (v) caro (a2).
- Wide streets are less dangerous. – Ruas (s) largas (a1) são (v) menos perigosas (a2).
- The new computer ended up more expensive. – O computador (s) novo (a1) ficou (v) mais caro (a2).

➤ In a statement-question:

If you want to ask a question in Portuguese, the Portuguese word order is the same as when you make a statement. All you have to do is to raise the intonation at the end to make it sound like a question. However, pay attention to the fact that whereas in English you need to use a verb at the beginning when you ask a question, in Portuguese you don't need to. So, if it helps, when you are transferring your thoughts from English into Portuguese, try to imagine that you could ask questions in English without the words "do", "are" or "will", etc., at the beginning of a question. For instance, in English, you would say "Are you gentlemen going to schedule a meeting for tomorrow?" whereas in Portuguese you would say "Os senhores vão marcar a reunião para amanhã?". For you to understand the correct Portuguese word order, let's observe the same phrases used above as examples, now turned into questions.

Subject > Verb > Object > Phrase Complement

- Does he have a house in Rio de Janeiro? – Ele (s) tem (v) uma casa (o) no Rio de Janeiro (pc)?
- Did she wash her clothes in the washing machine? – Ela (s) lavou (v) a roupa (o) na máquina de lavar (pc)?
- Did we read a book at the beach? – Nós (s) lemos (v) um livro (o) na praia (pc)?
- Are they having salmon for lunch? – Eles (s) comem (v) salmão (o) ao almoço (pc)?

➤ In a direct question:

You basically keep the normal structure of a statement, then adding a question word at the beginning, and obviously raising the intonation at the end. Let's, once again, look at some examples.

Subject > Verb > Object

- What does he do in Rio de Janeiro? – O que (é que) ele (s) faz (v) no Rio de Janeiro (o)?

- Where did she wash her clothes? – Onde (é que) ela (s) lavou (v) a roupa (o)?
- Where do we read the book? – Onde (é que) nós (s) lemos (v) o livro (o)?
- What do they have for lunch? – O que (é que) eles (s) comem (v) ao almoço (o)?

➤ In negative form:

What you need to do to form a negative sentence is to place the negative word before the verb to get a correct Portuguese word order. Negative words are often "não" (no, don't), "nunca" (never), or "nem" (nor). Nevertheless, remember: the word order in Portuguese is still the same.

Subject > Negative locution > Verb > Object

- I don't want soup. – Eu (s) não (nl) quero (v) sopa (o).
- He never studied the word order. – Ele (s) nunca (nl) estudou (v) a ordem das palavras (o).
- We aren't going to the beach. – Nós (s) não (nl) vamos (v) à praia (o).
- They are not even going to have lunch at home. – Eles (s) nem (nl) vão (v) almoçar em casa (o).
- The milk is never fresh. – O leite (s) nunca (nl) é fresco (o).

Exercise

1) **Translate these sentences to Portuguese:**

a) What is your dog's name?

b) My dad has a green shirt.

c) I don't have a good laptop for gaming.

d) I want the vegetable soup.

2) **Ask the direct questions that originated these sentences** (E.g.: I prefer the strawberry ice cream. Which ice cream do you

prefer? = Eu prefiro o gelado de morango. – Qual é o gelado que preferes?):

  a) Eu vou à escola amanhã.

  b) É o meu pai que te vai buscar ao cinema.

  c) Eu sei isso porque estudei.

  d) A minha cor favorita é azul.

3) Write these sentences in the negative form:

  a) Eu quero ir correr!

  b) Tu gostas de camarão?

  c) Eles vêm connosco à praia.

  d) Vocês fazem sempre o que vos peço.

  e) Eu até sei muito sobre esse assunto.

Answers

2) Translations:

  a) Qual é o nome do teu cão?

  b) O meu pai tem uma camisa verde.

  c) Eu não tenho um computador bom para jogos.

  d) Eu quero a sopa de vegetais.

3) Questions4:

  e) Quando vais à escola?

  f) Quem me vai buscar ao cinema?

  g) Como sabes isso?

  h) Qual é a tua cor favorita?

4) Negative:

  i) Eu não quero ir correr.

  j) Tu não gostas de camarão?

---

4 The solution to this exercise presents some examples that are accepted; there are, however, many other possible answers.

k) Eles não vêm connosco à praia.

l) Vocês nunca fazem o que vos peço. / Vocês fazem sempre o que não vos peço.

m) Eu até nem sei muito sobre esse assunto.

Determiners

The determiners are elements of the language which are placed before the noun and that identify or determine what the noun refers to. They differ from the pronouns in the sense that pronouns substitute nouns, whereas determiners, as said previously, precede them. Check out this example, so it becomes clearer:

- A *minha* mãe é alta! – My mom is tall!
- A *minha* também é! – Mine is as well!

In the first sentence, the word "minha" precede the noun "mãe"; therefore it is a determiner. In the second sentence, the word "minha" works as a substitute for "mãe"; hence it is a pronoun.

There are six different types of determiners, and we are going to study them all. Bear in mind that in Portuguese, the determiners must agree in gender and number with the noun. Later on, we will also approach the pronouns to see how to use and identify them. Be aware that many words are used both as determiners and pronouns, depending on the context. So, whenever you're doing some reading, try to identify the noun in the sentence, so you can more accurately determine what the word is referring to.

➤ **Possessive determiners:**
- Meu / minha (my); meus / minhas;
- Teu / tua (your); teus /tuas;
- Seu / sua (her/his); seus / suas;
- Nosso; nossa (our) / nossos; nossas;
- Vosso / vossa (your); vossos; vossas;
- Seu / sua (their); seus /suas.

These exist to indicate possession regarding someone or something. For instance:

- My shirt is blue. – A *minha* camisa é azul.

➤ Demonstrative determiners:

- Este / esta (this); estes / estas (these);
- Esse / essa (that); esses / essas (those);
- Aquele / aquela (that); aqueles /aquelas (those);
- Isto (this, or this thing right here);
- Isso (that, or that thing – further away than "this", but closer than "aquilo");
- Aquilo (that thing over there).

These exist to identify and indicate the position, whether in time or space, of someone or something. For instance:

- This is my house. – Esta é a minha casa.

➤ Indefinite determiners[5]:

- Todo / toda (all); todos / todas;
- Algum / alguma (any, something); alguns / algumas (some);
- Nenhum/ nenhuma (none); nenhuns / nenhumas;
- Outro / outra (other); outros / outras (others);
- Muito / muita (a lot, many, quite); muitos / muitas (many);
- Pouco / pouca (little, not much); poucos / poucas (few);
- Tanto / tanta (much/such); tantos / tantas (many);
- Qualquer (any); quaisquer;
- Tudo (everything);
- Nada (nothing);
- Cada (each);
- Ninguém (no one/nobody);

---

[5] The English translations to the indefinite determiners are not totally accurate, at least not for every situation—since the English word might change depending on what is being said, even if the Portuguese term is the same in those different sentences.

- Alguém (someone/somebody).

These exist to refer to being or things in an imprecise way. For instance:

- I'm going to call somebody to come here. – Vou chamar alguém para vir cá.

➤ Quantifiers and interrogative determiners:

- Qual (which one); quais (which ones);
- Quanto / quanta (how much); quantos / quantas (how many);
- Que (what);
- Quem (who, whom).

These exist to introduce interrogations, or when we're in need of giving someone information about the number or amount of something. For instance:

- What is the price? – Qual é o preço?
- How many flowers are in the jar? – Quantas flores estão no jarro?

➤ Pre-determiners:

- Cujo / cuja (which); cujos/ cujas (whose);
- Quanto / quanta (how much); quantos/ quantas (how many);
- Qual (which); quais (which ones);
- Que (what);
- Quem (who, whom).

These are used to express the opinion about the noun they modify. For instance:

- What a sunny day! – *Que* dia tão solarengo!

Articles

The determiners "the", and "a" or "an" are translated to Portuguese as "o", "a", "os", "as" and "um", "uma", "uns", "umas". Language experts call these words "articles", which are words that come before nouns and are used to define their gender. In Portuguese, just like in the English language, there are two types of articles: the definite articles—"o", "a", "os", "as"—and the indefinite articles—"um", "uma", "uns", and "umas". The reason that there are four representations of both types of articles in Portuguese is because there is a distinction between the masculine and feminine words, and between the singular and plural. Let's see how they are used in some sentences.

➤ **The definite article:**

The definite article implies that something is one thing, or a specific thing, or several specific things. It is, as the name implies, something that is defined or determined already. In Portuguese, the word "o" corresponds to a masculine singular noun, and the word "os" corresponds to a masculine, plural noun, where the word "a" corresponds to a feminine singular noun, and the word "as" corresponds to a feminine plural noun:

- O bolo de aniversário – The birthday cake.
- Os bolos de aniversário – The birthday cakes
- A bola de futebol – The soccer ball
- As bolas de futebol – The soccer balls

➤ **The indefinite article:**

The indefinite article implies that something is one undetermined or unspecified thing, among others of the same kind. The word "um" corresponds to a masculine, singular noun, and the word "uns" corresponds to a masculine, plural noun, whereas the word "uma" corresponds to a feminine, singular noun, and the word "umas" corresponds to a feminine, plural noun.

- Um bolo de aniversário – A birthday cake
- Uns bolos de aniversário – Some birthday cakes
- Uma bola de futebol – A soccer ball
- Umas bolas de futebol – Some soccer balls

Exercise

1) Identify the determiners in the following sentences:

a) O jardineiro tratou do meu jardim.

b) Estas flores exigem cuidados.

c) Aquela fila do teatro está reservada para a nossa equipa.

d) Que trabalho vais fazer?

2) Fill in the blanks with either definite or indefinite articles:

a) Fui ao cinema e vi _____ bom filme. Estava lá _____ meu amigo João, que me convidou para ir ver _____ filme, que era _____ filme preferido dele. _____ meus amigos da escola queriam ver outra coisa, então foram para _____ casa da Maria. Ela preparou _____ tostas com queijo.

3) Which sentences have a determiner on it? Write down the determiner:

a) Eu gosto muito dele.

b) Aquela casa é a minha.

c) Este é o meu irmão.

d) O jardineiro tratou-me disso.

Answers

1) a) meu; b) estas; c) aquela, nossa; d) que

2) a) Fui ao cinema e vi *um* bom filme. Estava lá *o* meu amigo João, que me convidou para ir ver *um* filme, que era *o* filme preferido dele. *Os* meus amigos da escola queriam ver outra coisa, então foram para *a* casa da Maria. Ela preparou *umas* tostas com queijo.

3) b) aquela; c) meu

Verbs and Tenses

In Portuguese, verbs are conjugated according to their endings. There are three different ways of conjugating them:

- The first form or conjugation includes all regular verbs ending in "ar";
- The second conjugation includes all regular verbs ending in "er";
- And the third conjugation includes all regular verbs ending in "ir".

As in any other language, there are also irregular verbs in Portuguese, which are not included in those three ways of conjugating verbs. To conjugate a verb in the present tense you take the verb, separate the stem (take out its ending—"ar", "er", or "ir"), and then you add the endings which are specific for this tense.

A quick, and *extremely important*, note before we start: the two verbs "**ser**" and "**estar**" are both a translation of to the verb "to be" in English, but each verb is used in different situations. The difference lies in the fact that "**ser**" is used, generally, when we are referring to more permanent states. For example, to talk about height, type of body, nationality, and things of this nature, i.e., things that are unlikely[6] to change in our lives, the verb "**ser**" is used. On the other hand, if you are talking about states that are likely to suffer changes, the verb "**estar**" is used. If you want to say something about the way you feel at a certain moment, how the weather is on a specific day, or other things that will probably change in no time, you'll use this form of the verb "to be". Let's take a look at a few examples:

- Eu sou alta. – I am tall.
- Eu estou contente. – I am happy.
- Eu sou loira. – I am blonde.
- Eu tenho 20 anos. – I am 20 years old.

---

[6] Just a fun fact – if you want to say "I'm married" in Portuguese, you would have to use the verb "ser" – "Eu *sou* casado/a". And that is because even though it is not a permanent state, historically, once you got married, that likely wouldn't ever change.

Present Tense

> ## Verbs ending in "ar":

For the verbs ending in "ar", you add the following endings to their stem—"o", "as", "a", "amos", "ais", and "am". For instance:

- Verb "to love" – amar, stem – am;
  - o Present of amar: Eu amo, Tu amas, Ele/ela ama, Nós amamos, Vós[7] amais, Eles amam;
- Verb "to sing" – cantar, stem – cant;
  - o Present of cantar: Eu canto, Tu cantas, Ele/ela canta, Nós cantamos, Vós cantais, cantam;
- Verb "to speak" – falar, stem – fal;
  - o Present of falar: Eu falo, Tu falas, Ele/ela fala, Nós falamos, Vós falais, Eles falam.

> ## Verbs ending in "er":

For the verbs that end in "er" in the present tense, you add the following endings to their stem—"o", "es", "e", "emos", "eis", and "em". For instance:

- Verb "to eat" – comer, stem – com;
- Present of comer: Eu como, Tu comes, Ele/ela come, Nós comemos, Vós comeis, Eles comem;
- Verb "to live" – viver, stem – viv;
- Present of viver: Eu vivo, Tu vives, Ele/ela vive, Nós vivemos, Vós viveis, Eles vivem;
- Verb "to fear" – temer, stem – tem;
- Present of temer: Eu temo, Tu temes, Ele/ela teme, Nós tememos, Vós temeis, Eles temem.

> ## Verbs ending in "ir":

---

[7] "Vós", which corresponds to the second person plural, is rarely used nowadays. What you will hear 99% of the times in written and/or spoken form is the word "vocês", which means the same thing. However, there's a catch—if you use "vocês", you have to conjugate the verb as if it were in the third person plural.

To conjugate the verbs that end in "ir" in the present tense, you add the following endings to their stem—"o", "es", "e", "imos", "is", and "em". For instance:

- Verb "to leave" – partir, stem – part;
- Present of partir: Eu parto, Tu partes, Ele/ela parte, Nós partimos, Vós partis, Eles partem;
- Verb "to insist" – insistir, stem – insist;
- Present of insistir: Eu insisto, Tu insistes, Ele/ela insiste, Nós insistimos, Vós insistis, Eles insistem;
- Verb "to fullfil" – cumprir, stem –cumpr;
- Present of cumprir: Eu cumpro, Tu cumpres, Ele/ela cumpre, Nós cumprimos, Vós cumpris, Eles cumprem.

Past Tense

Now, we are going to focus on the Past Simple tense, referred to in Portuguese as "passado perfeito", which is used to refer to actions that happened or were completed in the recent past. The Past Simple refers to completed actions that had a definite beginning and a definite end. As you know by now, in Portuguese there are three different classes of verbs: the verbs ending in "ar", the verbs ending in "er", and the verbs ending in "ir". Each class of regular verbs has its own pattern of termination when conjugated in the past. When conjugating regular verbs in the simple past form, you just have to preserve the root of the verb and substitute "ar", "er" or "ir" for the following terminations:

- Verb "to love" – amar, stem – am
    o Past simple of amar: Eu amei, Tu amaste, Ele/ela amou, Nós amámos, Vós amastes, Eles amaram;
- Verb "to run" – correr, stem – corr;
    o Past simple of correr: Eu corri, Tu correste, Ele/ela correu, Nós corremos, Vós correstes, Eles correram;
- Verb "to feel" – sentir, stem – sent;
    o Past simple of sentir: Eu senti, Tu sentiste, Ele/ela sentiu, Nós sentimos, Vós sentistes, Eles sentiram;

For verbs ending in "gar" and "car", the first person—"eu"—is conjugated using the termination "guei" and "quei", as you can see in the following examples:

- Verb "to arrive" – chegar, stem – cheg;
    - o Past simple of chegar: Eu cheguei, Tu chegaste, Ele/ela chegou, Nós chegámos, Vós chegastes, Eles chegaram;
- Verb "to stay" – ficar, stem – fic;
    - o Past simple of ficar: Eu fiquei, Tu ficaste, Ele/ela ficou, Nós ficámos, Vós ficastes, Eles ficaram;

Future Tense

Let's switch to the future now. The simplest of all of the future tenses is simply known as 'future' or 'future of the indicative', which is the one we are going to study for now. In English, this tense is achieved by using the auxiliary verb "will", or sometimes "shall". In Portuguese, however, the future tense is not used very often in oral communication, especially if it is informal. You are more likely to come across the future indicative in writing than in speech. The true future indicative is a simple form, and is conjugated as follows:

- Verb "to work" – trabalhar, stem – trabalh
    - o Future indicative of trabalhar: Eu trabalharei, Tu trabalharás, Ele/ela trabalhará, Nós trabalharemos, Vós trabalhareis, Eles trabalharão;
- Verb "to think" – pensar, stem – pens;
    - o Future indicative of pensar: Eu pensarei, Tu pensarás, Ele/ela pensará, Nós pensaremos, Vós pensareis, Eles pensarão;
- Verb "to eat" – comer, stem – com;
    - o Future indicative of comer: Eu comerei, Tu comerás, Ele/ela comerá, Nós comeremos, Vós comereis, Eles comerão;
- Verb "to write" – escrever, stem – escrev

o Future indicative of escrever: Eu escreverei, Tu escreverás, Ele/ela escreverá, Nós escreveremos, Vós escrevereis, Eles escreverão;

- Verb "to guarantee" – garantir, stem – garant;
  o Future indicative of garantir: Eu garantirei, Tu garantirás, Ele/ela garantirá, Nós garantiremos, Vós garantireis, Eles garantirão;
- Verb "to attend" – assistir, stem – assist;
  o Future indicative of assistir: Eu assistirei, Tu assistirás, Ele/ela assistirá, Nós assistiremos, Vós assistireis, Eles assistirão;

However, not all verbs follow these rules. Here are a few examples of the conjugation of irregular verbs:

- Verb "to be" – estar, stem – est
  o Future indicative of estar: Eu estarei, Tu estarás, Ele/ela estará, Nós estaremos, Vós estareis, Eles estarão;
- Verb "to be" – ser, stem – ser;
  o Future indicative of ser: Eu serei, Tu serás, Ele/ela será, Nós seremos, Vós sereis, Eles serão;
- Verb "to go" – ir, stem – ir;
  o Future indicative of ir: Eu irei, Tu irás, Ele/ela irá, Nós iremos, Vós ireis, Eles irão;

A helpful hint for remembering the future indicative forms is that they all start with the full infinitive—not just the stem of it (although not all irregular verbs do so). Be careful, though, not to confuse the third person plural form of the future indicative with the past third person plural, as they both start with the full infinitive.

Exercise

1) <u>Conjugate the verb "lançar" in the present tense.</u>

2) <u>Conjugate the verb "beber" in the future tense.</u>

3) <u>Conjugate the verb "sorrir" in the simple past tense.</u>

4) Rewrite these sentences in the simple past tense:

    a) Eu como um gelado.

    b) Eu gosto muito deste filme.

    c) Ele não morre tão facilmente.

5) Rewrite these sentences in the future tense:

    a) Eu vou à praia amanhã.

    b) Ele está preparado par ao teste.

    c) Nós fazemos isto.

Answers

1) Eu lanço, tu lanças, ele/ela lança, nós lançamos, vós lançais, eles lançam.

2) Eu beberei, tu beberás, ele/ela beberá, nós beberemos, vós bebereis, eles beberão.

3) Eu sorri, tu sorriste, ele/ela sorriu, nós sorrimos, vós sorristes, eles sorriram.

4) a) Eu comi um gelado. b) Eu gostei muito deste filme. c) Ele não morreu tão facilmente.

5) a) Eu irei à praia amanhã. b) Ele estará preparado para o teste. c) Nós faremos isto.

Adjectives

In Portuguese, an adjective must agree in gender and number with the word it is describing. Most of the time it is accompanied by a form of the verb "to be": either "ser" or "estar". Therefore, when you want to use an adjective to describe a word in Portuguese, you need to take into consideration whether it's in the masculine or feminine form and whether it's in the plural or singular, to then make the necessary adjustment—if any is needed. Another thing to consider is the form of the verb you're going to use. If you're describing an intrinsic quality or characteristic—which is something that is part of the noun you're talking about—you need to use the verb "ser". If you're describing a temporary condition or state of the noun you're talking about, you need to use the verb "estar".

➤ Here are some examples of an intrinsic quality:
- The blanket is green. – A manta *é* verde.
- João is stubborn. – O João *é* teimoso.
- Carla is stubborn. – A Carla é teimosa.
- Marina's eyes are blue. – Os olhos da Marina são azuis.

➤ Here are some examples of a temporary condition or state:
- The children are sick. – As crianças estão doentes.
- The dog is happy. – O cão está alegre.
- I am not okay. – Eu não estou bem.

Adverbs

An adverb is a word that can modify or characterize an action. In Portuguese, adverbs are varied in their forms and context to express time, place, mode, quantity, intensity, affirmation, denial, doubt and exclusivity. They can modify and adapt to:

- A verb;
- An adjective;
- Another adverb.

Now we will give you a small list of several adverbs from the different types mentioned above. It would obviously be impossible to name them all, especially with Portuguese being such a rich language, but adverbs are very important since they help you express yourself and get your message across in a much more effective way. Reading will definitely help you master these.

➤ **Adverbs that indicate time**:
- Immediately – Imediatemente
- Constantly – Constantemente

➤ **Adverbs that indicate place:**
- Here – Aqui
- Above – Acima

> **Adverbs that indicate mode or manner:**
>   - Quickly – Depressa/Rapidamente
>   - Easily – Facilmente
> **Adverbs that indicate quantity or intensity:**
>   - Very– Muito
>   - Little – Pouco
>   - More – Mais
>   - Less – Menos
> **Adverbs that indicate affirmation:**
>   - Certainly – Certamente
>   - Surely – Decerto
> **Adverbs that indicate denial:**
>   - Never – Nunca
>   - Neither – Nem
>   - Never ever – Jamais
> **Adverbs that indicate doubt:**
>   - Maybe – Talvez
>   - Probably – Provavelmente
> **Adverbs that indicate exclusivity:**

Only – Somente
  - Otherwise – SenãoPronouns

Pronouns exist to replace other words, either names or nouns. A pronoun, when used, makes your speech and conversation sound more natural and fluent, and at the same time, it breaks the boredom of repetition and redundancy. For instance, when you are introduced to somebody by a friend, you may have learned that you must say "Prazer em conhecê-lo/a", which means "Nice to meet you". In this case, the letters "lo/la" substitute the name of the person that you are referring to—so that is one example of a personal pronoun.

There are many different types of pronouns—the same types that there are in the determiners' category. We are going to, however, focus on the personal pronouns, more specifically in the direct object pronouns, and the indirect object pronouns, for now, to know how to use those and identify them in sentences.

> **Personal pronouns:**
>   o **Direct object pronouns:**

These are the pronouns that will lead you to the questions: "what" – "o quê" –, and "who" – "quem". For instance, take a look at this sentence:

- I'm dating Pedro. – Eu estou a namorar com o Pedro.

In this situation, you would ask "who are you dating?" The answer would be "Pedro." So that's the noun you are going to substitute for the pronoun. It would look like this:

- I'm dating him. – Eu estou a namorar com ele.

There are only eight pronouns under the direct object pronouns category:

- "Me" = which corresponds to the word "me" in English;
- "Te" = which corresponds to the word "you" in English;
- "O" = which corresponds to the word "him" or "it" when the object is masculine;
- "A" = which corresponds to the word "her" or "it" when the object is feminine;
- "Nos" = which corresponds to the word "us";
- "Vos", or "Vocês" = which corresponds to the plural of "you", just like the expression "you guys";
- "Os" = which corresponds to a masculine "them", be it people or objects;
- "As" = which also corresponds to a feminine "them" in English, be it people or objects.

Here are some rules to follow almost all of the time:

1) The pronoun comes after the verb, separated by a hyphen. For instance:

- I ate all of the ice cream. – Eu comi o gelado todo. = Eu comi-o todo.

2) The pronoun needs to be placed before the verb when the verb comes after, in five different situations:

- **Adverbs** – I also ate the ice cream. – Eu **também** comi o gelado = Eu também *o* comi.
- **Negatives** – I didn't eat the ice cream. – Eu **não** comi o gelado. = Eu não *o* comi.
- **Interrogations** – Who ate the ice cream? – **Quem** comeu o gelado? = Quem *o* comeu?
- **Relative pronouns** – He said he ate all of the ice cream. – Ele disse **que** comeu o gelado todo. = Ele disse que *o* comeu todo.
- **Prepositions** – She likes eating the ice cream with a spoon. – Ela gosta **de** comer o gelado com uma colher. = Ela gosta de *o* comer com uma colher.

3) If the verb ends with the letters "s", "z", or "r", the last letters of the verb fall and you add an "l" to the beginning of the pronouns "o" "a", "os" or "as". For instance:

- I'm going to do the portrait. – Eu vou fazer o retrato. = Eu vou fazê-*lo*.

4) When the verb ends with a nasal sound, keep the verb as it is and add "n" to the pronoun. For instance:

- They drink all of the wine. – Eles bebem o vinho todo = Eles bebem-*no* todo"

o **Indirect object pronouns:**

These are the pronouns that will lead you to the question "to whom", which in Portuguese has two forms – "A quem" and "Para quem". Bear in mind that if you're not able to ask "a quem" or "para quem", (to whom), and instead, the pronoun leads you to the question "quem" (who), you're not dealing with an indirect object, but instead with a direct object.

Again, we only have eight indirect object pronouns. Here they are:

- "Me"= which corresponds to the words "to me" in English;
- "Te"= which corresponds to the words "to you" in English;
- "Lhe"= which corresponds to the words "to him" or "to it" when the object is masculine;
- "Lhe"= which corresponds to the words "to her" or "to it" when the object is feminine;
- "Nos"= which corresponds to the words "to us";
- "Vos", or "para vocês" = which corresponds to the plural "to you", just like the expression "to you guys";
- "Lhes"= which corresponds to a masculine "to them", whether it is referring to people or objects;
- "Lhes" = which corresponds to a feminine "to them", whether it is referring to people or objects.

These obey the same rules the direct object pronouns do in terms of where they are placed in a sentence—whether it is before or after the verb. In other words, they normally come after the verb separated by a hyphen. For instance:

- I'm going to give Mário the book. – Eu vou dar o livro ao Mário. = Eu vou-lhe dar o livro.

The exceptions—when pronouns come before the verb—are also the same as before, and that happens when we have:

1) Adverbs:
   a) I also called Paulo. – Eu **também** telefonei para o Paulo. = Eu também *lhe* telefonei.
2) Negative statements:
   a) He doesn't call Paulo. – Ele **não** telefona para o Paulo. = Ele não *lhe* telefona.
3) Interrogations:
   a) Who called Paulo today? – **Quem** telefonou para o Paulo hoje? = Quem *lhe* telefonou hoje?
4) Relative pronouns:

a) He said he hit Pedro. – Ele disse **que** bateu no Pedro. = Ele disse que *lhe* bateu.

5) Prepositions:

a) She asked them to bring a coffee to him. – Ela disse **para** eles trazerem um café **para** ele. = Ela disse-*lhes* para *lhe* trazerem um café.

   o **Direct and indirect object pronouns:**

When we have both direct and indirect object pronouns together in a sentence, this is what you should do:

- He gave it to me. – Ele deu-me o livro. = Ele deu-mo.
- He gave it to you. – Ele deu-te o livro. = Ele deu-to.
- He gave it to him. – Ele deu-lhe o livro. = Ele deu-lho.

Exercise

1) Complete the blank spaces with the definite object:

   a) Eu vou preparar o jantar às sete da noite. – Eu vou … às sete da noite.

   b) Não vi os seus óculos. – Não … vi.

   c) Eles compraram os bilhetes hoje. – Eles … hoje.

   d) Vocês convidaram a Maria e o Carlos? – Vocês …?

   e) Eu fechei as janelas todas. – Eu … todas.

   f) Ele põe os pratos na mesa. – Ele … na mesa.

   g) Ela já leu o jornal? – Ela já …?

   h) Você quer fazer o exercício? – Você …?

   i) José comprou um presente ontem. – O José … ontem.

   j) Nós vimos as meninas na festa. – Nós … na festa.

2) Complete the blank spaces with the indefinite object:

   a) Quem disse isso ao Manuel e à Sofia? – Quem … isso?

   b) Ela trouxe esse livro para nós. – Ela … esse livro.

   c) Eles já entregaram a carta para a Maria? – Eles já … a carta?

   d) Nós demos um bonito presente de Natal ao José. – Nós … um bonito presente de Natal.

e) A Maria ligou para você hoje às 3 horas. – A Maria … hoje às 3 horas.

3) Rewrite the whole sentences using the pronouns you know:

    a) O João trouxe-me o caderno hoje.

    b) A Catarina não vem fazer o bolo.

    c) Eu dei ao Carlos o presente anteontem.

    d) Os pintores pintaram a casa ontem.

6) Identify the pronouns and determiners in the following sentence:

    Esta casa é a minha casa. Aquela é a tua.

Answers

1) Definite object:

    a) Eu vou prepará-lo às sete da noite.

    b) Não os vi.

    c) Eles compraram-nos hoje.

    d) Vocês convidaram-nos?

    e) Eu fechei-as todas.

    f) Ele põe-nos na mesa.

    g) Ela já o leu?

    h) Você quer fazê-lo?

    i) O José comprou-o ontem.

    j) Nós vimo-las na festa.

2) Indefinite object:

    a) Quem lhes disse isso?

    b) Ela trouxe-nos esse livro.

    c) Eles já lhe entregaram a carta?

    d) Nós demos-lhe um bonito presente de Natal.

    e) A Maria ligou-lhe hoje às 3 horas.

3) Definite and indefinite object:

    a) Ele trouxe-mo hoje.

    b) Ela não o vem fazer.

    c) Eu dei-lho anteontem.

    d) Eles pintaram-na ontem.

4) Pronouns and determiners:

Esta – demonstrative determiner; Minha – possessive determiner;
Aquela – demonstrative pronoun; Tua – possessive pronoun

Chapter 3 – Short Stories
#1 – The Beginning

Foi num solarengo dia de verão que os irmãos, Ana e Francisco, entraram num táxi rumo à estação de comboios da Gare do Oriente. Era lá que se tinham combinado encontrar com o seu grupo de amigos para apanhar o comboio que os iria levar até às suas tão desejadas férias no Algarve. Chegaram finalmente à linha de onde o comboio iria partir, e o resto do grupo já estava todo à sua espera.

It was on a sunny summer day that the siblings, Ana and Francisco, got into a taxi headed to the train station Gare do Oriente. It was there that they were going to meet with their group of friends to catch the train that would take them to their desired holiday in the Algarve. They finally arrived at the line from which the train would leave, and the rest of the group was already waiting.

> - Finalmente! Estava a ver que não chegavam a tempo – disse Mário, o namorado de Ana.
> - Olá para ti também! – respondeu Ana com um sorriso, ao mesmo tempo que dava a Mário um abraço.
> - Bom dia! Todos tranquilos que há muito tempo ainda! – atirou Francisco, sempre sem pressas.

- Bom dia não, é mais boa tarde! Têm sorte que o comboio também está atrasado e ainda não chegou. Devia estar aqui às 9h28, e já são 9h31. Costuma ser pontual, ao contrário de vocês. Mas desta vez a sorte esteve do vosso lado! É que se o perdessem, não tinham outra opção senão ir de autocarro. É que com a quantidade de gente que está aqui para ir para o Algarve hoje, não conseguiam bilhete de certeza! – exclamou Teresa.

- É verdade. O meu primo também vai ao festival e quis comprar bilhete para hoje à noite e já não havia nada. Só conseguiu para amanhã de manhã. – acrescentou Rui.

- Finally! I thought you'd not make it in time. – said Mário, Ana's boyfriend.

- Hello to you too! – Ana replied with a smile, at the same time giving Mário a hug.

- Good morning! Relax, there's still a lot of time! – said Francisco, always calm.

- Not good morning, it's almost good afternoon! You're lucky that the train is also late and has not yet arrived. It should have been here at 9:28 am, and it's now 9:31 am. It's usually on time, unlike you. But this time, luck was on your side! Because, if you had missed it, you would have no choice but to take the bus. And with the amount of people that are here to go to the Algarve today, you couldn't get a ticket! – said Teresa.

- That's true. My cousin is also going to the festival and wanted to buy a ticket for tonight, and there was nothing. He only managed to get one for tomorrow morning. – added Rui.

Este era um grupo de amigos que se conhecia de já há muito muito tempo. Os seus feitios, pese embora bastante diferentes, conjugavam muito bem entre si, o que fazia com que a sua amizade fosse verdadeira e muito pacífica, pelo menos a grande maioria das vezes. Tinham andados todos juntos na escola desde o ensino primário. Desde então nunca mais se quiseram separar. Depois de acabarem o

4°ano continuaram juntos, sempre na mesma escola e na mesma turma, pelo ensino secundário, e partilhando de interesses semelhantes, além de não suportarem a ideia de se separar, decidiram ir todos para a mesma licenciatura – a de Literatura Clássica – candidatando-se, naturalmente, para a mesma faculdade – a Faculdade de Letras da Universidade de Lisboa.

This was a group of friends who knew each other for a long time. Their personalities, although quite different, conjugated together very well among themselves, what caused their friendship to be genuine and very peaceful, at least the vast majority of the time. They all been in school together since first grade. Since then, they never wanted to go separate ways. After finishing the fourth grade, they continued together, always in the same school and in the same class in high school, and, due to sharing similar interests, and also because they couldn't stand the idea of separating, they then decided to take the same degree – Classic Literature – applying for, of course, the same college – the Faculty of Letters of the University of Lisbon.

A Ana e o Francisco eram irmãos gémeos. Surpreendentemente, sempre foram muito apegados um ao outro, e nunca tiveram a necessidade de se afastar. A sua relação era boa, com pequenas chatices e brigas, como é normal entre todos os irmãos, e eram muito cúmplices. No entanto, e apesar de serem gémeos, fisicamente não eram nada parecidos um ao outro. Ambos eram morenos, mas as suas semelhanças ficavam-se por aí. Ana tinha os olhos castanhos; Francisco tinha os olhos verdes claros. Francisco era alto e atlético; Ana baixa, e magra. Francisco tinha o nariz achatado, olhos em bico, e os lábios grossos e carnudos. Ana tinha os olhos grandes e redondos, o nariz pontiagudo, e a boca e lábios bem desenhados, mas finos. Quem os visse não adivinharia nunca que eram irmãos, quanto mais gémeos! Curioso era o facto de a Ana se parecer muito mais com a Teresa do que ao seu próprio irmão. Teresa tinha, tal como Ana, os olhos castanhos, mas ainda mais escuros. A Teresa também era baixa e magra, apesar de ser ligeiramente curvilínea. Também os seus narizes se assemelhavam bastante. Tinham as duas um nariz muito pontiagudo, embora não fosse comprido. O que definitivamente as distinguia era os seus cabelos: A Ana era morena, e tinha o cabelo liso e comprido. Teresa tinha uma farta, volumosa cabeleira loira, aos caracóis, que não passava do ombro. O Mário, o namorado de Ana, era o mais alto de todos do grupo. Ele não era gordo, mas tinha peso a mais. Os seus braços e pernas, tal como as suas mãos, eram longos. Usava óculos com uma lente tão grossa que os seus olhos aumentavam por detrás das lentes. O seu cabelo era preto, e parecia estar, impreterivelmente, sempre despenteado. O Rui, por outro lado, tinha um sedoso cabelo de cor castanha. O Rui era algo vaidoso, preocupava-se sempre em vestir-se bem, e estar bem arranjado. Era muito moreno, e os seus olhos eram pretos, de cor de azeitona.

Ana and Francisco were twins. Amazingly, they had always been very attached to each other, and never had the need to get away. Their relationship was good, with small troubles and fights, as it is normal between all brothers and sisters, and their chemistry was very good. However, and although they were twins, physically they weren't anything alike. Both were brunettes, but the similarities ended there. Ana had brown eyes; Francisco had light green eyes. Francisco was tall and athletic; Ana short and thin. Francisco had a flat nose, pointy eyes, and thick and fleshy lips. Ana had big round eyes, a sharp nose, and a beautifully drawn mouth and lips, but very thin. Whoever saw them would not guess that they were siblings, let alone twins! Curious was the fact that Ana looked more like Teresa than like her own brother. Teresa had, just like Ana, brown eyes, but even darker. Teresa was also short and thin, despite being slightly more curvaceous. Their noses were similar as well. She had a very pointy nose, although not long. What definitely distinguished them was the hair: Ana was a brunette, and her hair was straight and long. Teresa had bulky blonde hair, with lots of curls, which ended at her shoulders. Mário, Ana's boyfriend, was the tallest of all the people in the group. He was not fat but was slightly overweight. His arms and legs, just like his hands, were long. He wore glasses with such a thick lens that his eyes increased behind the lenses. His hair was black and seemed to be always unkempt. Rui, on the other hand, had silky brown hair. Rui was a bit vain, he always dressed well, and always looked good. He was very tanned, and his eyes were black, like an olive.

Entretanto, depois de a Ana e o Francisco terem chegado à estação, os amigos continuaram na galhofa até o comboio chegar, o que aconteceu não muito tempo depois. A viagem que iria demorar, de acordo com o previsto, 3 horas, era o início da aventura que tinha sido planeada ainda nos frios e longos meses de Inverno, por entre os corredores, salas de aula, e bibliotecas da Faculdade de Letras da Universidade de Lisboa. Na verdade, aquela ideia maluca tinha nascido vários meses antes, quando ainda faltava muito tempo para o Verão. Corria uma chuvosa e cinzenta terça-feira, no mês de Dezembro, quando o Rui viu no Facebook uma publicação do festival mais conhecido de Portugal—o Algarve Summer Fest—que iria decorrer no mês de Julho na bonita cidade de Tavira, no sul de Portugal. Eram apenas 8h53 da manhã, mas o seu cérebro pôs-se logo a pensar e o seu coração acelerou de imediato. Lembrou-se nesse instante dos seus amigos e fez o resto do caminho até à sala onde iria ter a primeira aula do dia a correr a galope. Assim que chegou ao anfiteatro, sentou-se ao pé dos seus amigos e logo lhes contou o que tinha visto.

Meanwhile, after Ana and Francisco arrived at the station, the friends continued joking around until the train arrived, which happened not long after. The journey that would take, according to the schedule, 3 hours, was the beginning of the adventure that had still been planned in the cold and long winter months, through the halls, classrooms, and libraries of the Faculty of Letters of the University of Lisbon. In fact, that crazy idea was born several months before, while the summer was still very far away. It was a gray and rainy Tuesday in December when Rui saw a Facebook post about the most popular festival in Portugal—the Algarve Summer

Fest—that would be held in July in the beautiful town of Tavira, in the south of Portugal. It was just 8:53 am, but his brain started thinking, and his heart sped up immediately. He thought of his friends right away and made the rest of the way to the classroom where he would have the first class of the day running at full speed. As soon as he arrived at the amphitheater, he sat by his friends and then told them about what he had just seen.

- Pessoal, vejam isto! – e mostrou-lhes o ecrã do telemóvel.
- Brutal, temos que ir! – disse o Francisco.
- Sim, sem dúvida. Já estou farta de estudar. Mas quando é? É que eu vou de férias com os meus pais em Agosto para o Norte, para a terra da minha mãe. – respondeu a Teresa.
- É em Julho, portanto não há problema. – disse-lhe o Rui.
- Então está combinado? Todos podem e todos vão? – perguntou logo Francisco, já muito entusiasmado.
- Sim! – gritaram todos em uníssono, pondo o resto da sua turma toda a olhar para eles, indignados com o barulho.
- Guys, check this out! – and showed them the cell phone's screen.
- Cool, we got to go! – Francisco said.
- Yes, without a doubt. I'm tired of studying. But when is it? I'm going on a vacation with my parents in August to the North, to my mother's hometown. – replied Teresa.
- It's in July, so there's no problem. – Rui told her.
- It's settled then? Everyone can go and everyone will go? – asked Francisco right away, already very excited.
- Yes! – they all yelled in unison, making the rest of the class stare at them, outraged by the noise.

Quando as aulas acabaram nesse dia, todos os elementos do grupo se dirigiram para casa com grande entusiasmo. Estavam desejosos de ir perguntar aos seus pais se estes os deixavam ir ao festival no Verão. E claro, se autorizariam, além da ida, o orçamento.... Afinal, os custos iriam ser elevados. Estas miniférias incluíam comprar a entrada para o festival, os bilhetes de ida e volta de comboio, dinheiro para a estadia, alimentação, um ou outro imprevisto, e claro, alguns *souvenirs*. Assim, na viagem para casa, cada um ia repetindo e ensaiando na sua cabeça aquilo que diria aos pais quando chegassem a casa. Pensavam em qual seria, enfim, a melhor forma de os convencerem. Além desta preocupação que os assolava, estavam também receosos por sabor o que diriam os pais dos amigos pois de nada valia terem autorização para ir se houvesse alguém do grupo a ficar de fora.

When classes ended that day, all the elements of the group headed home with great enthusiasm. They were eager to go ask their parents if they would let them go to the festival in the summer. And, of course, if they were allowed, in addition to going, the budget ... After all, the costs would be high. These mini-vacations included buying an entry to the festival, the train round-trip tickets, money for the stay, food, money for one or another unforeseen event, and, of course, some *souvenirs*. So, on the trip home, each one was repeating and rehearsing in their head what they would say to their parents when they got home. They were thinking about what the best way would be to convince them. In addition to this concern that worried them, they were also fearing what their friends' parents would say because it wouldn't matter if they could go if somebody on the group couldn't.

Ao chegar a casa, todos tentaram comportar-se da melhor forma possível. Punham as suas melhores maneiras, cara mais meiga e jeitos mais doces, para conseguirem levar os pais a proferir o tão ansiado "sim!". Nenhum deles foi corajoso ao ponto de fazer a pergunta ao chegar a casa. Todos esperaram a hora de jantar, para, em conversa amena e casual, lançarem a questão, como quem não quer a coisa. Apesar de terem esperado até à hora de comer para o fazer, não conseguiam deixar de pensar no assunto a cada segundo que passava. A Ana e o Francisco estavam particularmente nervosos, entreolhando-se constantemente. Foi então com grande entusiasmo e felicidade que mais tarde, ao trocarem mensagens no WhatsApp, puderam confirmar que os seus pais tinham acedido aos seus pedidos, e que assim, todos iriam, com certeza, passar juntos umas grandes férias, das quais, certamente, nunca mais se iriam esquecer!

When they got home, they all tried to behave in the best possible way. They prepared their best manners, sweetest face and softer ways, so they could lead their parents into uttering the much longed-for "yes!" None of them was brave enough to ask the question right when they got home. Everyone waited until dinner time, in warm and casual conversation to throw the question, like somebody who doesn't even care. Even though they waited until dinner time to do it, they could not help but think about it every second that passed. Ana and Francisco were particularly nervous, and they were looking at each other constantly. So it was with great excitement and happiness that later, when they exchanged messages on WhatsApp, they were able to confirm that their parents had accepted their requests, and so, they would certainly spend a great time together, of which they would never forget!

Questions

1) Where was the group of friends heading to?
2) Since when did the groups know each other?
3) Who found out about the event?
4) How did that person find out about the event?
5) Somebody had to check if they were free to go on a specific month. Who was it and which month would be a problem?
6) What worried the group when they were heading home after class?
7) Who in the group was particularly nervous?
8) How did the friends find out everyone else's parents had allowed them to go as well?

Answers

1)   To the Tavira, to attend the Algarve Summer Fest.
2) Since first grade.
3) Rui found out about it.

4) Through a Facebook post.

5) Teresa. She couldn't go in August because she would go on a vacation with her parents.

6) If their parents would not allow them to go.

7) The twins, Ana and Francisco.

8) Through a group chat in WhatsApp.

#2 – The First Day in Tavira

O grupo de amigos chegou à estação de comboios de Tavira ao final da manhã. A essa hora, todos eles estavam já esfomeados. A hora de almoço aproximava-se e a última vez que tinham comido tinha sido ao pequeno-almoço, várias horas antes. O entusiasmo da viagem tinha tapado as dores de estômago que a fome faz, mas agora que tinham chegado, não podiam deixar de as sentir. Assim que saíram do comboio, esperava-os um sol ainda mais quente do que aquele que os tinha deixado em Lisboa. Entusiasmadamente dirigiram-se à praça de táxis. A espera foi demorada, ou pelo menos assim lhes pareceu, já que estavam famintos. Ainda assim, de tão contentes que estavam, conseguiram ignorar o monstro que fazia barulhos esquisitos dentro dos estômagos deles.

The group of friends arrived at the Tavira's train station late in the morning. At that time, all of them were already hungry. The lunch hour was approaching and the last time they had eaten had been at breakfast, several hours before. The excitement of the trip had covered the stomachaches that hunger causes, but now that they had arrived, they couldn't stop feeling them. As soon as they got out of the train, awaiting them was a sun even hotter than the one that had left in them in Lisbon. Enthusiastically, they headed to the cabstand. The wait was a long one, or so it seemed to them, since they were really hungry. Nevertheless, they were so happy that they managed to ignore the monster that made weird noises inside their stomachs.

Já no táxi, e sem esconder a felicidade e o contentamento pelos dias de diversão que os esperavam, os amigos puderam ir vendo um pouco da maravilhosa cidade que os ia acolher durante praticamente uma semana. O céu sem nuvens deixava que o sol brilhasse claramente e iluminasse a paisagem. Viam-se alguns montes e planaltos, e bem lá ao fundo, filas infindáveis de laranjeiras e oliveiras. O verde seco, o laranja tijolo e alguns tons de castanho destacavam-se aos seus olhos. Eram as cores que dominavam o desenho que se lhes deparava. À medida que começaram a entrar numa zona mais urbana, mais residencial, começaram a ver casas pintadas a cal, muito tipicamente algarvias. Repararam também em alguns vestígios dos Mouros, que deixavam naquela terra, como em tantas outras, traços da sua identidade arquitectónica, mas não só. Felizmente, também alguns vestígios da sua língua perduraram na riquíssima língua Portuguesa. Em palavras como Algarve, Albufeira (que antes era Albuhera), Aljezur, Alfarroba, Alcácer do Sal, Almeirim, a influência é notória. O AL é um prefixo árabe—pelo menos foi o que aprenderam os amigos com o taxista que lhes ia ensinando um pouco da História do Sul da Península Ibérica. Assim, pensavam eles, já tinham algo interessante para contar aos pais quando voltassem.

In the cab, and without hiding the happiness and excitement due to the days of fun that were awaiting them, the friends were able to see a bit of the beautiful city that would receive them for almost a week. The cloudless sky let the sun shine clearly and illuminate the landscape. They could see some small hills and plateaus, and right there in the background, endless rows of orange and olive trees. Tones of dry green, brick orange and some shades of brown just jumped to their eyes. Those were the colors that dominated the painting that lay before them. As they began to get into a more urban, more residential area, they began to see houses painted with lime, very typical in the Algarve. They also noticed some traces of the Moors' heritage, who left, in that land, as so many others, traces of their architectural identity, but not only that. Fortunately, some traces of their idiom stuck to the rich Portuguese language. In words such as Algarve, Albufeira (formerly Albuhera), Aljezur, Alfarroba, Alcácer do Sal, Almeirim, the influence is notorious. AL is an

Arabic prefix—at least that's what the friends learned from the driver, who was teaching them a bit of the history of the South of the Iberian Peninsula. Well, so they thought, now they had something interesting to tell their parents when they got back.

O grupo de amigos, de tão excitado que ia, ia acenando aos residentes e vários turistas que com eles se iam cruzando. Estes, vagarosamente se turistas, apressadamente se residentes, seguiam as suas vidas, mas frequentemente acenavam de volta perante um grupo de jovens tão bem-disposto. Como a fome já não podia esperar mais, perguntaram ao taxista onde poderiam encontrar um bom restaurante perto do hotel, onde se comessem pratos típicos da cidade.

The group of friends were so excited that they were waving to the residents and to the several tourists they were coming across. These persons, walking slowly if tourists, quickly if residents, kept going on with their lives, but often waved back before such a cheerful group of young people. Since the hunger couldn't wait any longer, they asked the driver where they could find a good restaurant nearby to the hotel, where they could eat typical dishes of the city.

- Podem ir ao 5 Mares. É mesmo ao pé do hotel. Basta descer as escadas para a praia e virarem à direita depois da esquina. Não há nada que enganar. É o meu restaurante favorito. Aconselhava-vos a cataplana de marisco. É de morrer e chorar por mais. Só de pensar que lhe sinto o sabor. – disse o taxista, olhando para o vazio, com a boca a salivar.
- Muito obrigada, caro senhor! – agradeceu a Teresa.
- Pode-nos dizer quanto tempo demoramos a pé? – perguntou ainda o Francisco.
- Com certeza! Em menos de 10 minutos põem-se lá, sem dúvida. – respondeu o taxista, prontamente.
- You can go to "5 Mares". It is right by the hotel. Just down the stairs to the beach and turn right around the corner. It's easy-peasy. It's my favorite restaurant. I advise you to order the shellfish *cataplana*. It is to die for. Just thinking about it

and I can taste it. – said the taxi driver, looking away, his mouth salivating.

- Thank you so much, dear sir! – thanked Teresa.

- Can you tell us how long it'll take us to walk there? – asked Francisco.

- For sure! In less than 10 minutes you're there, no doubt. – promptly replied the taxi driver.

Assim fez o grupo de amigos. Depois de fazerem o check-in no hotel, e deixarem as malas nos quartos, dirigiram-se para o restaurante, prontos a saborear o que de melhor a gastronomia algarvia tinha para oferecer. Saíram do hotel e seguiram o caminho indicado pelo taxista. Mas, das duas uma: ou o taxista lhes deu o caminho errado, ou eles enganaram-se porque o que acabou por acontecer foi que o grupo se perdeu e acabou à deriva pelas ruas de Tavira, que, naturalmente, não conheciam. Já tinham passado praticamente 20 minutos, e nem sinal do restaurante 5 Mares. Com dores de barriga por estarem cheios de fome, e dores de cabeça pela paciência que ia escasseando, o ambiente no grupo começou a ficar ligeiramente mais tenso. As gargalhadas e risos que ainda há pouco se ouviam tinham-se agora transformado em silêncio. Não seguiam exactamente ninguém—iam como que deambulando todos em grupo, com a esperança de encontrarem o restaurante por milagre. Até que o Mário, de todos o mais stressado, ansioso e com mau-feitio, perdeu o pouco de paciência que tinha e explodiu:

And so, they did. After checking in at the hotel, and leaving the bags in the rooms, they headed to the restaurant, ready to enjoy the best gastronomy Algarve had to offer. They left the hotel and followed the path indicated by the taxi driver. But either the cab driver gave them the wrong way, or they screwed up because what ended up happening was that the group got lost and ended up drifting through the streets of Tavira, which of course, they did not know. 20 minutes had nearly passed, and no sign of the restaurant 5 Mares. With tummy aches, because they were starving, and headaches due to the patience that was going to down the drain, the mood in the group started to become a little tenser. The laughter that was heard moments ago had now turned into silence. They weren't following anyone exactly—they were walking as a group, towards nowhere, but all with the hope of finding the restaurant as a miracle. Then Mário, of all the most stressful, anxious and bad-tempered, lost what little patience he had and exploded:

- Não aguento mais, tenho fome e estou cansado. Não percebo porque não entramos num táxi e lhe pedimos para nos levar até lá! – disse, quase em gritos.

- Mário, já te dissemos porquê! Estamos a trabalhar com um orçamento pequeno e modesto, caso não te lembres, e temos que tentar poupar ao máximo, até para podermos gastar naquilo que vale realmente a pena! – respondeu a Ana.

- Opá, não estejam para aí a stressar! Não se chateiem; que a gente há-de chegar lá. Mas também se não chegarmos lá nos próximos minutos sem problema nenhum—comemos no primeiro restaurante que nos aparecer à frente. O que acham da ideia? – tentou ajudar o Francisco. – Mal fora se nos fôssemos agora chatear por causa disto e estragar as férias?

- Sim, o Francisco tem razão. Não vale a pena perdermos a paciência por causa disto. Além disso, estamos com fome, o que não ajuda a discutir nem a pensar para descobrir o caminho. –acrescentou a Teresa.

- Tenho outra ideia: vamos para a praça de táxi e perguntamos lá as direcções a um deles. De certeza que ninguém nos vai negar essa ajuda, e assim também não gastamos dinheiro. Eu tenho visto várias placas que indicam que há uma praça naquela direcção. Não parece faltar muito, por isso eu acho que é a nossa melhor hipótese! Que me dizem? – propôs o Rui, animado.

- Sim, pode ser... – respondeu o Mário, meio contrariado e ainda com a cabeça a olhar para o chão.

- É uma boa ideia, vamos lá! – tentou motivar a Teresa.

- I can't take this anymore, I'm hungry and I'm tired. I don't understand why we don't get in a cab and ask to get us there. – he said, almost shouting.

- Mário, I already told you why! We are working with a small and modest budget, if you don't remember, and we have to try to save as much as possible, at least to be able to spend on what is really worth it! – replied Ana.

- Hey, don't stress about it! Don't get upset over this; we will get there. But even if we don't get there in the next few minutes, it's not a problem—we'll eat in the first restaurant that appears in front of us. What do you think of the idea? – Francisco tried to help. – How stupid would it be if we got mad because of it and ruined the holiday?

- Yes, Francisco is right. It's not worth losing our patience over this. Plus, we're hungry, which doesn't help when trying to discuss things or think. – added Teresa.

- I have another idea: let's go to the taxi square and ask directions to one of them. I'm sure nobody will deny us that help, and we don't have to spend any money. I have seen several signs that indicate that there is a square in that direction. Doesn't seem to be very far away, so I think it's our best chance. What do you say? – proposed Rui, cheerfully.

- Yes, we can do that ... – Mário replied, a little upset and still looking down.

- It's a good idea, let's go! – said Teresa, trying to motivate everyone else.

Já a caminho da praça de táxis, os ânimos não pareciam ter atenuado muito. O grupo continuava maioritariamente em silêncio, com a excepção do Francisco, que ora ia cantarolando, ora assobiando, ora dizendo umas piadas tontas para tentar animar o grupo e aliviar a situação, que se tinha tornado então um pouco constrangedora. A culpada era na verdade a fome, pois aquela má-disposição provoca o mau-feitio. No entanto, ninguém parecia ficar contagiado pela onda de bom humor que o Francisco tentava espalhar. A Teresa, por educação e simpatia, ia sorrindo sempre que Francisco tentava algo novo, mas não o fazia genuinamente. Até o Rui parecia completamente desmotivado e abatido pela falta de comida. Nem a ideia de que em breve iriam, possivelmente, encontrar as indicações para o restaurante mudavam alguma coisa. Na cabeça deles, à excepção, claro, do Francisco, iam chegar ao pé do taxista apenas para ouvirem ou que o taxista não sabia onde era o restaurante, ou que era muito longe, ou que estava fechado naquele dia. Imaginavam mil desfechos, e todos eles maus.

Already on the way to the taxi stand, the tension did not seem to have faded a bit. The group kept mostly silent, with the exception of Francisco, who was humming, whistling, or saying some silly jokes to try to cheer up the group and cool down the situation, which had become slightly awkward. The culprit was actually hunger, because that bad mood causes bad temper. However, no one seemed to be infected by the wave of good mood that Francisco was trying to spread. Teresa, politely and friendly, would smile whenever Francisco tried something new, but she would not do it genuinely. Rui looked completely demotivated and weary from the lack of food. Even the thought that soon they would, possibly, find directions to the restaurant changed anything. On their heads, with the exception, of course, of Francisco, they would talk to a taxi driver just to hear from him that he didn't know where the restaurant was, or that it was too far, or that it was closed that day. They imagined a thousand outcomes, and all of them bad.

Assim continuaram os amigos durante alguns minutos. Com a excepção, claro, do Francisco, cabisbaixos e calados, rumo ao seu "trágico" e inútil destino. Não fosse Francisco ser um rapaz que não se desmotiva facilmente, aquele dia teria, sem dúvida, acabado mal. Ao passar uma ruela apertada que iria levá-los à praça de táxis, o Francisco, que ia olhando distraidamente em seu redor, avistou um letreiro meio empoeirado que dizia algo que não conseguia distinguir claramente, mas que lhe parecia ser engraçado.

So, the friends continued walking for a few minutes. With the exception, of course, of Francisco, they were all sad and quiet, walking towards their "tragic" and useless destination. If Francisco wasn't a boy who hardly gets discouraged, that day would have, undoubtedly, ended badly. When passing a tight alley that would take them to the taxi stand, Francisco, who was looking around distractedly, spotted a slightly dusty sign that said something that he couldn't quite read, but which seemed to be funny.

- Olhem o que diz ali: 5 Males! Devia ser o nome do nosso grupo neste momento específico—já que somos 5 e está tudo tão mal!... – disse o Francisco, que logo começa a rir sem parar.
- Look what it says there: 5 Evils8! It should be the name of our group at this particular time—since we're 5 and everything is so bad! ... – said Francisco, who immediately started to laugh non-stop.

O Mário, que foi o único que olhou, embora quase por instinto, e que estava pronto para mandar o Francisco calar-se, por estar farto de o ouvir a ele e à sua boa-disposição, leu o que estava na placa.

Mário, who was the only one who looked, although almost by instinct, and who was ready to tell Francisco to shut up, because he was tired of hearing him and his good mood, read what was on the board.

- Francisco, és um santo! Salvaste-nos! Mas és um santo tonto porque nem sequer te apercebeste do que acabaste de fazer, e quase íamos seguindo sem reparar nisto! É o restaurante! Não é 5 Males, mas sim *5 Mares*! – gritou o Mário, não cabendo em si de contente.
- Francisco, you are a saint! You saved us! But you're a foolish saint because you don't even know what you just did, and we were almost going to keep on moving without

<hr>

8 In Portuguese, the original name of the restaurant was "5 Mares" which means "5 Seas". When changing the "r" to "l", we've got "5 Males", which means "5 Evils".

noticing it! It's the restaurant! It's not 5 Evils, but 5 Seas instead! – shouted Mario, ecstatic.

O resto do grupo olhou imediatamente para cima e em direcção ao letreiro. Durante um segundo e meio, ficaram pasmados, sem perceber nada. A fome, mais uma vez, estava a atrasar-lhes a capacidade de raciocínio. Mas depois, os seus sorrisos foram-se formando, a sua tensão aliviando, o corpo relaxando... A energia, que parecia absolutamente esgotada ainda há instantes, voltou, inexplicavelmente, e logo se puseram todos aos saltos e a abraçar Francisco. Também a boa-disposição, que parecia só existir no Francisco, imediatamente contagiou todos, e a felicidade de estarem a começar uma grande aventura voltou. A fome, claro, ainda lá estava, mas foi esquecida durante uns minutos. O grupo começou então a dirigir-se para o restaurante, num ambiente livre de tensão, onde já só se ouviam gargalhadas e conversas animadas, sobre o que iriam escolher para comer. A verdade é que a fome aumentava à medida que sentiam os cheiros da gastronomia Algarvia a emanarem daquele sítio, mas sentiam-se tão contentes depois de tudo o que tinham passado, que já não sentiam essas dores. A paciência e a força estavam redobradas—e, por isso, ficaram eternamente agradecidos ao Francisco.

The rest of the group looked up and towards the sign. For a second and a half, they just stood still, without ever realizing what was going on. Hunger, once again, was keeping them from thinking. But then, their smiles started forming, their tension relieving, the body relaxing ... The energy, which seemed absolutely drained a few moments ago, came back, inexplicably, and soon, all were jumping up and down and hugging Francisco. Also, the good mood, which seemed to only exist in Francisco, immediately reached everyone, and the happiness of being at the start of a great adventure was back. The hunger, of course, was still there but was forgotten for a few minutes. The group then began heading for the restaurant, in a tension-free environment, and what could only be heard was laughter and joyful conversations about what they'd choose to eat. The truth is that hunger increased as the odor of the Algarve's gastronomy started to emanate from that place, but they felt so happy after what had just passed, that they no longer felt that pain. The patience and strength were redoubled—and, because of that, they were eternally grateful to Francisco.

Questions

1) In the first line of the story, a demonstrative pronoun is used. Which word is it?

2) In which tense is this verb conjugated "ficaram" (line 183)?

3) Grammatically, what is "nossa" (line 105)?

4) "Apressadamente" (line 44) is what grammatically? What would be the verb, noun, and adjective of the same word?

5) In the third line of the last paragraph, we can see the verbs "aliviar", "formar", and "relaxar" conjugated. In which tense?

6) "Francisco, és um santo!"(line 166) Rewrite this sentence in the future tense and in the past simple tense.

7) 5 Mares is the taxi driver's favorite restaurant. Which is the word that indicates that it is *his* favorite restaurant? How is that word referred to grammatically?

8) "Pode-nos dizer quanto tempo demoramos a pé?"(line 58) Can you identify a pronoun in this sentence? Of which type?

Answers

1) "Essa".

2) In the past simple tense, in the indicative form (In Portuguese, "pretérito perfeito, no modo indicativo").

3) A possessive pronoun.

4) Na – adverb of manner; Verb – Apressar; Noun – Pressa; Adjective – Apressado.

5) In the gerund.

6) Francisco, serás um santo. Francisco, foste um santo.

7) "meu" is a possessive determiner.

8) "nos" is a personal pronoun, more specifically, a direct object pronoun.

#3 – At the Algarve Summer Fest

- Não acredito que aqui estamos! – disse a Ana.
- É verdade. Sabe tão bem estar aqui com vocês, não é? – acrescentou a Teresa.
- A companhia não podia ser melhor! – disse o Rui. – São as minhas férias de sonho! E só agora começaram!
- O melhor ainda está para vir… – atirou o Francisco.
- Sabes que mais? Acho que tens razão! – concluiu o Mário.
- I can't believe we're here! – said Anna.
- It's true. It feels so good to be here with all of you, doesn't it? – added Teresa.
- And the company couldn't have been better! – said Rui. – These are my dream vacations! And they have just started!
- The best is yet to come... – said Francisco.
- You know what? I think you're right! – concluded Mario.

Todos estavam encantados com o pouco que tinham visto da cidade, do hotel, com o restaurante e a sua comida. Tudo o que tinham visto, provado, vivido, experimentado até agora tinha sido fantástico. Por isso mesmo, o Mário andava sempre com uma câmara fotográfica nas mãos, não fosse ele perder a chance de capturar algum momento único. No entanto, todos os momentos até agora lhe tinham parecido merecedores de captura, e então o Mário quase não falava com os amigos, tão focado que estava em arranjar os melhores ângulos para as suas fotografias.

Everyone was delighted with the little they had seen of the city, with the hotel, with the restaurant and its food. All that they had seen, tasted, lived, and experienced so far had been fantastic. Because of that, Mário was always with a camera in his hands, just so he wouldn't lose the chance of capturing a single moment. However, every moment until now had seemed worthy of capture, and so Mário almost didn't talk with his friends, so focused that he was on finding the best angles for his photos.

- Mário, tens que parar de tirar fotografias e aproveitar um bocadinho o que estamos a viver. Se estiveres só com a câmara a tirar fotos para depois relembrares estes momentos, não vais ter momentos para relembrar, e só os vais viver através do papel de fotografia... – disse-lhe a sua namorada.

- Depois do festival, até vários anos a seguir, todos me vão agradecer este esforço. Não vai haver nada melhor que estarem a ver fotos destes momentos tão especiais. E claro, para isso acontecer, há sempre alguém que tem que se sacrificar e andar sempre com a máquina fotográfica atrás! – respondeu-lhe o Mário.

- Eu não acho que seja bem assim, Mário! Nós até te podemos ficar gratos, mas tu vais ficar ressentido connosco porque o que vais levar daqui em termos de memórias vai ser muito pouco comparado connosco. Deixa isso e vive um bocadinho! Não é preciso tirar foto a absolutamente tudo... – disse a Teresa.

- Poxa! Vocês são chatos! Pronto, está bem, eu não tiro mais fotos... – cedeu o Mário por fim.

- Mário, you have to stop taking pictures and enjoy a little bit what we're living. If you're only with the camera taking pictures to remember these moments afterward, then you're not going to have any moments to remember, and you will live through the photographic paper only – his girlfriend told him.

- After the festival, and many years to come, everybody will thank me for this effort. There won't be anything better than being able to see the pictures of these special moments. And of course, for that to happen, there is always someone who has to sacrifice himself and be with the camera all the time. – answered Mário.

- I don't think it's quite like that, Mário! We can even be grateful, but you're going to hold a grudge against us because what are you going to take from here in terms of memories will be very small compared to us. Leave it be and live a little! There's no need to get absolutely everything on the camera... – said Teresa.

- Damn! You guys are annoying! Okay, I won't take any more pictures ... – said Mário, finally giving up.

O grupo já estava no recinto do festival. Absolutamente extasiados por estarem ali, e finalmente, que nem sabiam onde queriam ir primeiro. Este grupo de estudantes tinha esperado tanto tempo, ou pelo menos assim lhes tinha parecido, que agora que estavam mesmo lá, não conseguiam tomar nenhuma decisão. Ficaram ali todos especados, a olhar de fora para todo o frenesim de máquinas e infraestruturas montadas nas proximidades. Era algo realmente estrondoso e impactante. Decidiram ir para o fim da fila que os levava ao balcão da entrada, para que pudessem entrar dentro do recinto onde iam decorrer todas as actividades. Depois de ter passado pela entrada, onde validaram os seus bilhetes e lhe deram as pulseiras que teriam de usar durante todo o festival para poderem entrar e sair do recinto sem problemas, começaram a dirigir-se para o interior. Era cedo ainda – 3 da tarde – e ainda tinham muito tempo até ao primeiro concerto. No entanto, queriam ir entrando e adiantando as coisas, para não se atrasarem e correrem o risco de perder alguma coisa, fosse o que fosse. Além do mais, tinham que montar as tendas, e isso não se avizinhava ser uma tarefa fácil. Nenhum deles tinha alguma vez montado uma tenda, pelo que se mostravam um pouco preocupados.

The group was already on the festival grounds. Absolutely thrilled to be there, and finally, they didn't even know where they wanted to go first. This group of students had waited for so long, or at least that's what it seemed like, that now that they were there, they couldn't make a decision. They all stood there, staring at all the frenzy of the machines and facilities built nearby. It was something really stunning and impactful. They decided to go to the end of the line that led to the reception counter, so they could get inside the festival grounds, where all the activities were going to happen. After passing through the entrance, where they validated their tickets and were given the bracelets that they would have to use throughout the festival to be able to get in and out of the precinct without any problems, they headed inside. It was early still – 3 pm – so they had a lot of time until the first concert. However, they wanted to go in and start getting ahead of things, so they wouldn't be late and risk missing something, whatever it was. Besides, they had to set up tents, and it was a task that was going to be far from easy. None of them had ever pitched a tent, which was why they were a little worried.

Assim que começaram a caminhar pelo interior do recinto, perceberam logo que não ia ser uma tarefa nada fácil. O espaço, que até era bastante grande, estava cheio de gente já, e estava a ser difícil encontrar um sítio perfeito para poderem montar as suas tendas. Muita juventude já se tinha antecipado a eles, e ido mais cedo do que eles. Naturalmente, tinham escolhido os melhores lugares para eles, e já não havia muitas opções decentes. Apesar disso, o grupo não desanimou, e eventualmente, lá encontraram um espacinho até bastante agradável e plano, à sombra e à beira de um pequeno ribeiro, para poderem começar aquele próximo desafio. Tiraram as tendas das mochilas e puseram mãos à obra. Estacas voavam pelo ar, pedras serviam de martelos—a confusão reinava. Apesar de ninguém saber como montar tendas, ninguém teve a brilhante ideia de ler as instruções, até que a Teresa os lembrou disso. Escusado será dizer que até ao final do festival fizeram piadas com o facto de terem passado tanto tempo a montar uma tenda, para depois de lerem as instruções, o fazerem em 10 minutos.

As soon as they began walking through the grounds, they realized it wasn't going to be an easy task. The space, which was quite large, was already crowded, and it was hard to find a perfect place to set up their tents. A lot of young people had already anticipated them and arrived sooner than they had. Of course, they had chosen the best places for themselves, and there were no longer many decent options. Despite this, the group was not discouraged, and eventually, they found a spot that was quite nice and flat, in the shade and by a small stream, where they could start the next challenge. They took the tents out of their backpacks and started working. The tent spikes were flying through the air, stones served as hammers—confusion reigned. Although no one knew how to set up tents, no one had the bright idea to read the instructions, until Theresa reminded them of that. Needless to say, until the end of the festival, they all made jokes about the fact that they spent so much time trying to pitch a tent, to later, after reading the instructions, doing it in 10 minutes.

Umas horas, muito suor, e milhões de partículas de poeira levantadas, as tendas estavam montadas, e puderam sentar-se e descansar por uns momentos. Não quiseram, no entanto, perder muito tempo, pois queriam começar a divertir-se. Decidiram comer qualquer coisa para recuperar a energia e ir dar uma volta pelo recinto para ver que actividades e concertos iam haver naquela noite.

A couple of hours, a lot of sweat, and millions of dust particles later, the tents were assembled, and they were able to sit and rest for a while. They did not want to waste much time, however, because they wanted to start having fun. They decided to eat something to regain their energy and go for a walk around the grounds to see what activities and concerts were going to take place that night.

- Oh! Vai tocar o meu cantor favorito em menos de 15 minutos! Façam o que quiserem, mas em 5 minutos, eu vou começar a ir para lá! – avisou o Rui.
- Calma, Rui! A gente vai contigo! Como é que ele se chama mesmo? – perguntou o Francisco.
- Carlos Pompeu! É um grande poeta! – respondeu-lhe o Rui.
- Poeta? Então, mas isto não é um festival de música? Ou vimos para aqui ouvir recitais de poesia? – disse a Ana a brincar e a tentar provocar o Rui.
- Oh, Ana, usa os miolos! Ele não é um escritor, um poeta literalmente. Mas escreve letras lindíssimas, é liricista, autor, como lhe queiras chamar, e faz canções muito tocantes. Por isso, é nesse sentido que digo que é um grande poeta, que escreve grande poemas. – respondeu o Rui.

- Oh! My favorite singer is going to play in less than 15 minutes! Do what you want, but in 5 minutes, I'll start to go there! – warned Rui.
- Relax, Rui! We'll go with you! What's his name again? – asked Francisco.
- Carlos Pompeu. He's a great poet! – answered Rui.
- Poet? Isn't this a music festival? Or are we here to attend poetry recitals? – said Ana jokingly and trying to provoke Rui.
- Oh, Ana, use your brains! He's not a writer, a poet literally. But he writes beautiful lyrics, is a lyricist, author, whatever you want to call him, and makes very touching songs. So it is in that sense that I say that he is a great poet, who writes great poems. – replied Rui.

Todos conseguiram arranjar-se e ficar prontos dali a 5 minutos para irem ver o tão adorado cantor do Rui. Era apenas o primeiro concerto da noite, e planeavam assistir a todos, se a sua energia isso permitisse, independentemente de gostarem ou não. Por ser uma experiência que não queriam esquecer nunca, e pela incerteza de a voltarem a viver, não queriam desperdiçar nenhum momento nem faltar a nenhuma actividade. Queriam experimentar tudo e, num momento posterior, decidir e debater sobre aquilo que tinham gostado mais e menos. Mas, até ali, tudo lhes parecia igualmente perfeito, e único, inesquecível, memorável, inolvidável...

They were all able to get ready in 5 minutes to go see the beloved singer that Rui wanted to see. It was only the first concert of the night, and they planned to watch every single one of them, if their energy allowed it, regardless of whether they liked it or not. Due to it being an experience that they didn't want to ever forget, and also because of the uncertainty they would ever return, they didn't want to waste any time or miss any activity. They wanted to experience everything and, at a later moment, decide and discuss what they had enjoyed more and less. But, until that point, everything seemed perfect, and unique, unforgettable, memorable, indelible...

Questions

1) Write down the first three nouns that you find in the first paragraph that are feminine, and three in the second paragraph that are masculine.

2) What is the feminine form of the word "poet"?

3) Can you find, in the fourth paragraph, the first uniform noun (in Portuguese, "substantivo uniforme")?

4) What is the plural form of the word "papel"?

5) In the last line of the text you can find many adjectives together. What is their relation with each other?

6) On line 114, the word "literalmente" is used. What is that?

7) What would be the adjective equivalent to "literalmente"?

8) "Decidiram" is a word on line 102. In which tense is it?

9) Write down the previous verb in the infinitive form, and its adjective and noun equivalent.

Answers

1) Verdade; Companhia; Férias; Hotel, Restaurante, Momento.
2) Poetisa.
3) The noun "estudantes".
4) Papéis.
5) They are all synonyms of each other.
6) An adverb.
7) Literal.
8) Past tense.
9) Decidir. Adjective – decidido/a; Noun – decisão.

#4 – The Last Day

- Estou mortinho por dar um mergulho! – disse o Francisco.
- A quem o dizes… O sol queima como fogo! – concordou o Rui.
- Estás todo vermelho! Não puseste protector solar? És mesmo tonto! Eu tenho aqui se quiseres. – disse-lhe a Teresa.
- Ah! Não sabia que tinhas! – respondeu o Rui.
- Já tinha gritado para o mundo ouvir… Tu é que fizeste orelhas moucas[9]…. Queres ficar moreno, mas assim apanhaste um granda[10] escaldão… – disse a Teresa.
- Calmex[11], agora não vale a pena chorar sobre leite derramado… Eu sabia que tu me safavas; uma mulher prevenida vale por duas[12]. – atirou o Rui.
- Bem, tens razão. O que não tem remédio, remediado está. Vá, vem lá aqui para eu te por o creme nessas costas. Meu Deus…. Pareces uma lagosta ou um caranguejo. – disse ainda a Teresa.
- Opá e tu pareces uma lula, de tão branca que és. – provocou o Rui, a rir-se.
- I'm dying to dive in! – said Francisco.
- Tell me about it... The sun burns like fire! – agreed Rui.
- You're all red! You didn't put any sunscreen on? You are such a fool! I have it here if you want. – he told Teresa.
- Oh! I didn't know you had it! – answered Rui.
- I said that out loud for the world to hear ... You ignored it. You want to get a tan, but you just got yourself a sunburn... – said Teresa.
- Relax, now it's no use crying over spilled milk. And I knew you would save me; women are always prepared. – said Rui.

---

[9] "Mouco" means deaf. This expression literally means "making deaf ears", meaning, not hearing, intentionally, what someone said.
[10] It means "grande" (big). It is kind of like the logic between "a lot off" and "lotta".
[11] Slang for "Calma", which literally means "calm", and it has the intent of telling someone to calm down.
[12] Literally, "a prepared woman counts as two".

- Well, you're right. What has no solution, solved it is. Come on, come here so I can put the lotion on that back. My God ... You look like a lobster or a crab. – added Teresa.

- Hey, and you look like a squid, being as white as you are. – Rui provoked her, laughing.

Enquanto estes dois continuavam, distraidamente, à bulha, o Rui continuava ainda à procura do caminho para a praia. Iam andando e rindo, por todas as parvoíces que lhes saíam da boca. Poderia dizer-se que o Francisco, de todos o mais engraçado, ia particularmente inspirado:

While these two kept fighting distractedly, Rui was still looking for the right way to the beach. They were walking and laughing, due to all of the nonsense that was coming out of their mouths. It could be said that Francisco, the funniest of them all, was particularly inspired:

- Estavam duas cebolas numa panela a fumegar. E uma diz assim "Que calor!", e a outra vira-se e diz "Ha! Uma cebola que fala!" – diz ele, completamente às gargalhadas.

- Francisco, a sério, que piada tão seca! Ainda assim pões toda a gente à gargalhada! Tu és mesmo *de partir o coco a rir*![13] – disse, às gargalhadas, o Rui.

- Olha, se não nos concentrarmos, não vamos encontrar a praia. Eles devem estar preocupados! Ou então deliciados, por se livrarem de nós! – lembrou a Teresa.

- Bem, pelo que percebi do senhor da recepção, temos que subir aquela subida, depois virar à esquerda, em direcção a umas escadas, descê-las e já está. – disse Francisco, tentando ajudar.

- Pois, Francisco, complicado era descer uma subida... – brincou a Teresa.

- Oh, tu percebeste, oh chica esperta!

---

[13] Literally translated, it means "to crack a coconut while laughing".

- There were two onions in a boiling pot. And one says, "It's so hot!", and the other turns around and says "Ha! An onion that speaks!" – he says, completely in stitches.
- Francisco, seriously, what a lame joke! Yet you make everyone laugh! You are really funny! –said Rui, laughing.
- Look, if we don't focus, we won't find the beach. They must be worried! Or maybe delighted, for getting rid of us! – Teresa recalled.
- Well, from what I understood at the reception desk, we have to go up that hill, then turn left towards the stairs, get down, and that's it. – said Francisco, trying to help.
- Right, Francisco, it would be complicated to go down a hill... – joked Teresa.
- Oh, you know what I meant, smartass!

Entretanto, já iam avistando a praia. Era a primeira vez que lá iam, e logo no último dia de férias em Tavira. Como tinham montado a tenda perto de um pequeno ribeiro, e as noites tinham sido bastante activas e desgastantes, os dias eram aproveitados para dormir e descansar. Não lhes apetecia ter que andar para a praia quando podiam refrescar-se logo ali naquele ribeiro. No entanto, não queriam ir embora de Tavira sem visitar as suas famosas praias. Decidiram, então, no último dia que tinham, visitar a praia de Tavira. Estavam, pois, muito animados e entusiasmados, e nem o facto de estarem absolutamente esgotados e de ser o último dia ali lhes retirava a alegria e a boa-disposição.

Meanwhile, they started seeing the beach. It was the first time they went there, and right on the last day of holiday in Tavira. Since they had their tent near a small stream, and the nights had been quite active and exhausting, the days were used for sleep and rest. They didn't feel like having to walk to the beach when they could take a dip right there on that stream. Nevertheless, they didn't want to leave Tavira without visiting its famous beaches. They then decided that on the last day they would visit the beach of Tavira. They were, therefore, very excited and enthusiastic, and not even the fact they were absolutely exhausted, plus being the last day that they were there, affected their joy and good mood.

Quando finalmente chegaram à praia, o Rui, o Francisco, ea Teresa depararam-se com a árdua missão de encontrar o resto do grupo—o Mário e aAna. Estes dois tinham-se levantado um pouco mais cedo que os outros para irem dar uma volta e namorar um pouco a sós. Mas agora queriam encontrar-se e não viam como o iriam fazer. A praia estava cheia de pessoas, e nem Mário nem Ana atendiam o telemóvel.

When they finally reached the beach, Rui, Francisco, and Teresa faced the arduous task of finding the rest of the group—Mário and Ana. These two had gotten up slightly earlier than the others to go for a walk and to have a little alone time together. But now they wanted to meet and didn't know how to. The beach was full of people, and neither Mário nor Ana answered their cell phones.

> - Devem ter ido dar um mergulho... – assumiu a Teresa.
> - Eu é que vou dar um mergulho, não tarda nada! – atirou o Francisco, a suar em bica.
> - Eu acho é que aqueles comilões estão no bar a petiscar! – supôs o Rui. – Vamos lá ver!
> - Maybe they went for a swim... – assumed Teresa.
> - I am the one who is going to take a dip, in no time! – said Francisco, sweating profusely.
> - I think those hungry gannets are in the bar, having a snack. – assumed Rui. – Let's see!

E assim fizeram. A caminho do bar, o Francisco não aguentou e correu a toda a velocidade para dar um mergulho, voltando logo de seguida. Nem 3 minutos demorou. E afinal, o Rui tinha razão e conhecia os seus amigos como ninguém. Lá sentados estavam o Mário e a Ana, a comer uma sandes de queijo cada um. Também os recém-chegados decidiram sentar-se a comer. Aprenderam da experiência do primeiro dia que estar com fome não é nada boa ideia. E aquela aventura de Verão, prestes a terminar, acabava como tinha começado—com os amigos a sentarem-se num restaurante algarvio, com um grande sorriso na cara.

And so they did. On the way to the bar, Francisco gave in to the heat and ran at full speed to take a dip, returning right away. It didn't even take 3 minutes. And after all, Rui was right all along, and he really knew his friends like nobody else. Sitting there were Mário and Ana, each eating a cheese sandwich. The newcomers decided to sit down and eat as well. They had learned from the experience of the first day that being hungry is not a good idea. And that summer adventure in Tavira, which was about to end, ended how it began— with the friends sitting in an Algarve's restaurant, with a big smile on their faces.

Questions

1) In the second line, what figure of speech is used by Rui?

2) Can you identify any Portuguese saying or proverb in the first paragraph? Write it down.

3) Francisco tells a joke to Teresa and Rui. What figure of speech is used in it?

4) Teresa makes fun of Francisco for saying something a bit stupid. What is it?

5) Why was the group separated?

6) Can you find out, given the context, what the expression "de partir o coco a rir" on line 35 means?

Answers

1) A simile.

2) Orelhas moucas; Não vale a pena chorar sobre leite derramado; O que não tem remédio, remediado está.

3) Personification of the onion.

4) For saying "subir a subida", which in Portuguese is a pleonasm/redundancy.

5) Because Ana and Mário went to the beach earlier to be together alone for a bit.

6) It means that someone or something is so funny that you can even perform a very challenging task, like cracking a coconut, and laugh while doing it.

Chapter 4 – Basic sentences

In this chapter, you will find a small list of the most current words and sentences that you may hear if you visit a Portuguese-speaking country, or that you may need if you try to speak Portuguese for the first time. Be aware that the following lists are intentionally short. Many important words are missing—some you'll see on the pocket dictionary, others you might have read in the short stories, some might be somewhere in the adverb chapter, and others you'll find out by yourself. You are not expected to learn Portuguese by memorizing a bunch of pre-established dialogues. Instead, our goal in these pages is just to give you the absolute fundamental sentences that every language book presents their reader for their first contact with the language, and which can aid you if you're in a hassle in a Portuguese speaking country. We expect, however, that by the end of this book, you'll manage to build some sentences by yourself with no need to revisit this section of the book.

Starting out

My name is Pedro. – O meu nome é Pedro.

My favorite color is… – A minha cor preferida é...

My father is a driver. – O meu pai é condutor/motorista.

My mother is very young. – A minhã mãe é muito nova.

I have three brothers and one sister. – Eu tenho três irmãos e uma irmã.

I'm 25 years old. – Eu tenho 25 anos.

I'm fine! – Estou bem!

Let's go! – Vamos!

No. – Não.

What is your name? – Qual é o seu nome?

When is it? – Quando é?

Why? – Porquê?

Yes. – Sim.

Greetings

Everything okay? – Está tudo bem?

Good afternoon! – Boa tarde!

Good evening! – Boa noite!

Good morning! – Bom dia!

Goodbye! – Adeus / Xau[14]!

Have a nice day – Tenha um bom dia!

Hello! – Olá!

Hi! – Oi!

How are you? – Como está?

How have you been doing – Como tem passado?

See you later! – Até logo!

See you soon. – Até já.

---

[14] "Xau" is a very informal way to say goodbye, so use it only when speaking in an informal situation.

Thank you for your help! – Obrigado/a[15] pela sua ajuda.

Very well! – Muito bem!

You're welcome! – De nada.

Out and about

Can you help me, please? – Pode ajudar-me, por favor?

Can you repeat, please? – Pode repetir, por favor?

Can you translate for me? – Pode traduzir para mim?

Could you speak more slowly, please? – Podia falar mais devagar, por favor?

Could you write that down, please? – Pode escrever isso, por favor?

Do you speak English? – Fala Inglês?

Excuse me. – Com licença/Desculpe.

How do I get to…? – Como chego a…?

How much does this cost? – Quanto custa?

I don't speak portuguese very well. – Eu não falo Português muito bem.

I don't understand. – Não percebo/entendo.

I need to use the bathroom. – Desculpe, preciso de usar a casa de banho.

I need some help. – Eu preciso de ajuda.

I only speak English. – Eu só falo Inglês.

I understand. – Eu percebo/entendo.

I'm lost. – Estou perdido/a.

I'm not from around here. – Eu não sou daqui.

---

[15] You should use "Obrigado" if you're a man, and "Obrigada" if you're a woman—it doesn't matter who you're talking to.

I'm very thankful! – Eu estou muito agradecido/a!

I'm here on vacation. – Estou cá de férias.

I'm sorry. – Lamento/Desculpe.

Just a moment. – Um momento.

Let's go! – Vamos!

Nice to meet you! – Prazer em conhecê-lo/a!

No problem. – Sem problema/Não há problema.

Please say that again. – Por favor diga isso mais uma vez.

Please. – Por favor.

Regards! – Cumprimentos!

See you later! – Até logo!

See you soon! – Até já!

See you tomorrow! – Até amanhã!

Sure. – Claro/Com certeza.

Thank you! – Obrigado/a!

What does that mean? – O que significa isso?

What time does this place open/close? – A que horas abre/fecha?

What time is it? – Que horas são?

Where does this train/bus go? – Para onde vai esse comboio/autocarro?

Where is the bathroom? – Onde é a casa de banho?

Helpful Lists

In this chapter, we have prepared a few different sets of lists that may be helpful on several occasions. Just browse through them and come back whenever you deem fit.

PT vs. BR Portuguese

A few different words

As we have said, the Portuguese spoken in Portugal differs a little from the Portuguese spoken in Brazil. With that in mind, we have prepared a short list of several words that you may come across and not recognize. The word will be in English first, then translated in PT Portuguese, and then finally, in BR Portuguese.

Bathroom – Casa de banho / Banheiro

Boy – Rapaz / Moleque

Breakfast - Pequeno-almoço / Café da manhã

Bus – Autocarro/ Ônibus

Candy – Rebuçado / Bala

Cell phone – Telemóvel / Celular

City Hall – Câmara municipal / Prefeitura

Cool – Fixe / Legal

Draught beer – Imperial / Chope

Driver's licence – Carta de condução / Carteira de motorista

Flight attendant – Hospedeira de bordo / Aeromoça

Fridge – Frigorífico / Geladeira

Give a ride – Dar boleia / Dar carona

Grass – Relva / Gramado

Hello? (Answering the phone) – Estou sim? / Alô?

Ice cream – Gelado / Sorvete

Identity card – Bilhete de identidade / Cédula de identidade

Issue – Assunto / Negócio

Juice – Sumo / Suco

Line – Fila / Bicha

Money – Dinheiro / Grana

Nap – Sesta / Cochilo

Okay – Ok / Valeu, Tá

Police station – Esquadra da polícia / Delegacia

Sport – Desporto / Esporte

Subtitles – Dobragem / Doblagem

Suit – Fato / Terno

Team – Equipa / Time

To drive – Conduzir / Dirigir

To Shower – Tomar banho / Tomar uma ducha

Toilet seat – Sanita / Vaso

Train – Comboio / Trem

Tram – Eléctrico / Bonde

Truck – Camião / Caminhão

Underpants – Cuecas / Calcinha

Watercolor – Aguarela / Aquarela

Weight room – Ginásio / Academia

Different wording

> **Placement of the reflexive pronouns**:

Regarding the placement of the reflexive pronouns, in European Portuguese, the pronoun always comes after the verb. In Brazilian Portuguese, the tendency is usually to place the pronoun before the verb. Take a look at these examples:

- My name is André. – (PT) Eu chamo-*me* André. (BR) Eu *me* chamo André.

- Do you feel better today? – (PT) Você sente-*se* melhor hoje? (BR) Você *se* sente melhor hoje?

However, bear in mind that in negative sentences, in both PT and BR Portuguese, the pronoun always comes before the verb, like in these examples:

- My name is not André. – Eu não me chamo André.
- You don't feel better today? – Você não se sente melhor hoje?

➤ **nfinitive vs. Gerund:**

To describe something that someone is doing at this very moment, Portuguese and Brazilians use different tenses. In Portugal, they use the compound tense "estar a" plus the infinitive of the verb, whereas in Brazil, they replaced it with "estar" plus the gerund of the verb. Just take a look at these examples for it to become clearer:

- They are studying at home. – (PT) Eles estão a estudar em casa. (BR) Eles estão estudando em casa.
- While I'm cooking, my husband is taking a shower. – (PT) Enquanto eu estou a cozinhar, o meu marido *está a tomar* banho. (BR) Enquanto *estou cozinhando*, meu marido *está tomando* banho.

Common mistakes

In this list, we have compiled the most common mistakes among beginners and intermediate speakers and wrote it down for you. Some of them might have to do with the spelling of a word, others with grammar and the structure of the sentence, and some might be regarding the pronunciation. You should check out this list to correct the mistakes you might be making, or to avoid them in the future.

Grammar mistakes

➤ "Conhecer" vs "Encontrar"

These two verbs often create some confusion among beginners. Below, you will find a small explanation of the meaning of each verb and some examples to help clarify it.

"Conhecer" can mean:

- to meet someone for the first time, e.g., "I first met him when I was at the park." – "Eu conheci-o quando estava no parque".
- to know something which someone is talking about, eg., "Ah, yes. I know that restaurant." – "Ah, sim. Eu conheço esse restaurante."
- to know a place to which you have been before, e.g., "I know Japan." – "Eu conheço o Japão."
- "Encontrar" can mean:
- to meet someone that you knew before, e.g., "I met him again yesterday in the park." – "Eu encontrei-o outra vez ontem no parque."
- to find something, e.g., "I found a coin on the floor." – "Eu encontrei uma moeda no chão."

➤ "Poder" vs. "Conseguir":

In the same way, people who are just now starting to learn the language may find it difficult to know the difference between "poder" and "conseguir". Take a look at the following examples:

"Poder" can mean:

- to be allowed to do something, e.g., "I can go out until 1 am." – "Eu posso sair até à uma da manhã."
- to have the possibility, e.g., "I can look after your dog." – "Eu posso cuidar do teu cão."
- "Conseguir" can mean:
- to have the capacity to do something, e.g., "I can jump really high." – "Eu consigo saltar muito alto."

Tip: Both "poder" and "conseguir" are sometimes used interchangeably, but in general they take on the roles described above. The idea that "poder" is something like "can", while "conseguir" is something like "to manage" or "being able to", may help you differentiate the verbs. For instance:

- Can you pass me the water? – Pode chegar-me a água? (in a situation where you're just asking for somebody to pass you the water)
- Do you manage/are you able to pass me the water? – Consegue chegar-me a água? (in a situation where you're asking if somebody is able to do it—if for instance, the water bottle is on a high shelf.)

Incorrect spelling

➤ "Por que"/ "Porquê"/ "Porque"

These words work like the "why/because" pair. "Por que" and "Porquê" (why) are used to ask questions (implicit or explicit) and "Porque" (because) is used for answers. Take a look at the following examples:

- For what reason is he not here yet? – Por que motivo é que ele ainda não está aqui?
- Everything is dark. Why? – Está tudo escuro. Porquê?
- Marcos didn't come to work because he was sick. – Marcos não foi trabalhar porque estava doente.

Tip: "Porque" can almost every time be replaced by the word "pois", e.g.:

- I didn't go to the party because I didn't want to. – Não fui à festa porque/pois não quis.

➤ "Mal"/ "Mau"

"Mal" can be an adverb or a noun, and it is the opposite of "well", which means "bem". "Mau" (bad/evil) is an adjective. It is the opposite of "good", which means "bom".

- That smells very bad. – Aquilo cheira muito mal.
- My father drives well. – O meu pai conduz bem.
- I always wake up in a good mood. – Acordo sempre de bom humor.
- The dictator was a bad man. – O ditador foi um homem mau.

> ## "Mas"/ "Mais"

"Mas", which means "but", is a conjunction used to suggest contrast and "mais" is an adverb that means "more" and is the opposite of "less". Therefore, "mas" indicates opposition and "mais" indicates quantity. This mistake might happen especially in the spoken variation of Brazilian Portuguese. The Brazilian accent adds an "i" when saying "mas", which makes it seem that they're saying "mas". Nevertheless, you should be able to understand which one is being used based on the context.

- More beer, please. – Mais cerveja, por favor.
- I want to travel, but I don't have any money. – Quero viajar, mas não tenho dinheiro nenhum.
- The more I speak to her, the more I fall in love. – Quanto mais eu converso com ela, mais me apaixono.
- Clara did her best, but she didn't get the job. – Clara deu o seu melhor, mas não conseguiu o emprego.

> ## "Haver"/ "Existir"

The verb "haver", which means "there is" in the sense "to exist", has no plural form. So we can say:

- There was only one person at the bar. – Só *havia* uma pessoa no bar.

But if we are referring to a larger quantity, the verb remains in the singular:

- There were 30 people at the meeting. – Havia 30 pessoas na reunião.

- There are many ways to say "I love you." – Há várias maneiras de dizer "eu amo-te".
- There will be changes in the system. – Haverá mudanças no sistema.

➤ **"Obrigado"/ "Obrigada"**

This one is simple, but still, many people can slip up sometimes. As explained above, in Portuguese, women say "obrigada" and men say "obrigado", regardless of whomever they are speaking to.

➤ **"Meio-dia e meia" - right/ "Meio-dia e meio" - wrong**

12h30 pm reads "meio dia e meia", not "meio dia e meio", like it is usually, but wrongly, said. It is "mei*a*" (half), in the feminine form since it is referring to "*meia hora*" (half an hour). Hour, in Portuguese, is a feminine word. Therefore, saying "meio-dia e meia" is the abbreviation of "meio dia e meia hora", which would literally translate to something like "half a day plus half an hour". The same goes for 12h30 am, which would be "meia noite e meia" (literally— half a night plus half an hour).

➤ **"Descrição"/ "Discrição"**

With very similar pronunciations and written forms, "descrição" and "discrição" have very distinct meanings. "Descrição" means "description", while "discrição" means "discretion". So it's very important not to mix the two. Take a look at these examples to help clarify it:

- I appreciate your discretion when dealing with the issue. – Agradeço a sua discrição ao lidar com o assunto.
- The cops asked the victim for a description of the robber. – Os polícias pediram à vítima uma descrição do assaltante.

Tip: Maybe you have noticed that just like in the English language, one word has an "e" and the other has an "i". If you don't confuse the English words, you may use that clue to identify when to use each word.

➤ **"Sessão"/ "Secção"**

Here we have another case of two words that are written similarly, sound very much alike, but that might create some confusion since their meanings are very different. "Sessão" with two 's' means "session", and "secção" with the 'cç' means "section". For instance:

- Silence! The session is about to begin. – Silêncio! A sessão vai começar!
- Ice cream is found in the frozen section of the supermarket. – O gelado encontra-se na secção de congelados do supermercado.

➤ **"Aonde"/ "onde"**

Though both "aonde" and "onde" mean "where" in English, the word "aonde" suggests that someone is going somewhere, carrying the idea of movement and displacement, whereas "onde" indicates the place where something or someone is, being related to permanence. Take a look at these examples:

- Do you know where my keys are? – Sabes onde estão as minhas chaves?
- Where are you going? – Aonde vais?

➤ **"Trás"/ "traz"**

There is no distinction between them in spoken language—they sound the same. Nevertheless, their meanings differ significantly. "Trás" is an adverb of place that means "back", while always being preceded by a preposition, while "traz" is the correspondent of the verb "to bring", in the third person singular. See how it applies in the examples below:

- Money doesn't bring happiness. – Dinheiro não traz felicidade.
- There is no point in looking back now. – Não adianta olhar para trás agora.

Tip: More than any trick, mnemonic or memory clue, the context will help you decipher which word is being used and with what meaning. When writing, if you're having a tough time figuring out how to spell it, try conjugating the verb.

False Cognates

False cognates, or false friends, are words and terms that may look, sound or be written in a very similar way in both languages, but that have very different meanings. To help you out with these tricky words and sneaky friends, we have compiled a list of the most usual or known false cognates you may find throughout your Portuguese journey. However, before that, here are a few tips to help you recognize some of the false friends that won't be featured on this list:

➤ **Always check the meaning of new words:**

Never assume that two words that sound similar in English and Portuguese have the same meaning. Look up the new words and write down their correct meaning;

➤ **Learn false cognates with examples in context:**

Context is extremely important when you are learning vocabulary! Never learn a word without an example of how it is used. Context always helps us understand what words mean. Take two words that sound very similar in English and Portuguese, find one sample sentence for each and you will quickly see the difference in usage between them;

➤ **Practise with bad translations:**

Have you ever watched an English film with subtitles in Portuguese? Try to follow them and pick out the mistakes! There will be more than you think. You can also try this exercise with translated texts.

- Acesso = Access ‖ Assess = Avaliar
- Actualmente = Currently ‖ Actually = Na verdade, na realidade
- Advertir = to warn or advise ‖ Advertise = Publicitar

- Aluno = Student || Alumnus = Alumnus
- Amassar = To crush || Amass = Acumular
- Antena = Antenna || Anthem = Hino
- Aparelho = Equipment or apparatus || Apparel = Roupas
- Apontamento = Note || Appointment = Marcação
- Apreciação = Judgment, evaluation || Appreciation = Agradecimento, reconhecimento, gratidão
- Arma = Gun, weapon || Army = Exército
- Assistir = to watch (TV, for example) || Assist = Ajudar
- Assumir = to take over || Assume = Presumir
- Atender = Tend to, or to answer a call || Attend = Ir a, marcar presença
- Azar = Bad luck || Hazard = Risco, perigo
- Balcão = Counter (e.g. in a bar) || Balcony = Terraço
- Casualidade = Chance or coincidence || Casualty = Baixa, fatalidade
- Cigarro = Cigarette || Cigar = Charuto
- Colar = Necklace, or to glue || Collar = Colarinho, gola
- Colégio = Private School || College = Universidade, faculdade
- Compasso = Compasses || Compass = Bússola
- Compromisso = Commitment || Compromise = Entrar em acordo, fazer concessão, ceder
- Conceito = Concept || Conceit = Presunção
- Construir = To build || Construe = Interpretar
- Convicto = Convinced || Convict = Condenado
- Costume = Custom || Costume = Máscara, fato, fantasia
- Cota = Share, quota || Quote = Citar, citação
- Data = Date || Data = Dados
- Decepção = Disappointment || Deception = Fraude
- Dente = Tooth || Dent = Amassado
- Diversão = Fun || Diversion = Distracção, desvio
- Educado = Polite || Educated = Instruído, culto
- Esperto = Smart || Expert = Perito, especialista
- Esquisito = Strange || Exquisite = Belo, refinado

- Eventualmente = Possibly, maybe || Eventually = Finalmente, por fim
- Excitante = Arousing || Exciting = Empolgante
- Êxito = Success || Exit = Saída
- Fábrica = Factory || Fabric = tecido
- Físico = Physicist | |Physician = Médico clínico
- Gratuito = Gratuitous, free || Gratuity = Gorjeta
- Gripe = Flu || Grip = Agarrar
- Guitarra = Electric guitar || Guitar = Violão
- Hospício = Madhouse || Hospice = Abrigo para viajantes
- Ingenuidade = Naivety || Ingenuity = Creatividade, engenho
- Injúria = Insult || Injury = Lesão, ferida
- Jornal = Newspaper || Journal = Diário
- Lanche = Midday snack || Lunch = Almoço
- Largo = Broad, wide, or patio || Large = Grande
- Legenda = Subtitles || Legend = Lenda
- Leitura = Reading || Lecture = Conferência
- Livraria = Bookstore || Library = Biblioteca
- Maior = Bigger || Mayor = Prefeito
- Notícia = News || Notice = Observar, notar
- Ofício = Profession || Office = Escritório
- Parentes = Relatives || Parents = Pais
- Pasta = Folder, briefcase || Pasta = Massa
- Polícia = Police || Policy = Políticas
- Prejudicar = To harm, make damage || Prejudice = Preconceito
- Preservativo = Condom || Preservative = Conservante
- Pretender = Intend || Pretend = Fingir
- Próprio = Own || Proper = Adequado
- Puxar = Pull || Push = Empurrar
- Realizar = Accomplish, achieve || Realize = Perceber, dar-se conta
- Recipiente = Container || Recipient = Destinatário
- Recordar = to remember || Record = Gravação

- Resumir = Sum up, summarize || Resume = Recomeçar, retomar
- Retirar = Remove || Retire = Aposentar-se
- Rim = Kidney || Rim = Borda, beira
- Sapo = Toad || Sap = Seiva
- Sensato, ajuízado = Sensible || Sensitive = Sensível
- Suportar = to withstand || Support = Apoiar
- Taxa = Fee || Tax = Imposto

Terrível = Terrible || Terrific = ExcelenteNevertheless, there are also good cognates, true friends, on which we can rely on. If we follow a specific set of rules, there many words we can form directly from the English correspondent. For instance, the words that end in "ty" in English, transform to Portuguese easily, following one simple rule. The English suffix "ty" is equivalent to the Portuguese suffix "dade". So you just need to switch one for the other, while the rest of the word stays the same:

- Adversi-ty – adversi + dade = Adversidade
- Capacity = Capacidade
- City = Cidade
- Humanity = Humanidade
- Priority = Prioridade
- University = Universidade
- Velocity = Velocidade
- Simplicity = Simplicidade

With the words that end in "tion", we just need to switch it for "ção".

- Simplifica-tion = simplifica + ção = Simplificação
- Nation = Nação
- Observation = Observação
- Naturalization = Naturalização
- Sensatio = Sensação

For the adverbs of manner, which usually end in "lly", you just have to switch it for "mente".

- Natura-lly – natural + mente = Naturalmente
- Genetically = Geneticamente
- Orally = Oralmente
- Literally = Literalmente

In words that end with "ence", change that to "ência".

- Ess-ence – ess + ência = Essência
- Reverence = Reverência
- Frequence = Frequência
- Eloquence = Eloquência

Finally, or *finalmente*, many words that end in "al" in English are written the same way in Portuguese.

- Natural = Natural
- Total = Total
- General = General
- Fatal = Fatal
- Sensual = Sensual

There are, obviously, some exceptions, which don't exactly follow the rules. These set of rules work like a crutch—they are here to help you, but you're not supposed to rely on them all the time. To avoid making those types of mistakes, always double check what you're writing, and confirm the meaning and context.

Common idiomatic expressions, proverbs and sayings

Portuguese is a very old and rich language, so, naturally, it has its fair share of common expressions, proverbs, and sayings. In this list, we are going to focus on the most common or known expressions and proverbs that exist in the European Portuguese. Some of them might be applied and used in the other CPLP (Community of Portuguese Language Countries), with a slight or no variation, others might not be known at all—you can use them, though, and then brag about how you taught a native an expression he or she didn't know!

Also be aware that some expressions or proverbs have their translation, literal or not, in the English language. For those expressions that don't have one correspondent in the English language, its meaning will be explained.

'Bora! – Let's go! (Abreviation of the word embora, and used in situations where someone might say "vamos embora", but instead just says "bora")

A curiosidade matou o gato. – Curiosity killed the cat.

A dar com pau! – When there's a lot of something.

A esperança é a última a morrer. – Hope is the last thing to die.

A falar no diabo. – Speak of the devil.

À maneira. – It's great.

A mentira tem perna curta. – Literally, it means that a lie has short legs, meaning a lie can't go very far without being noticed.

A meu ver. – In my opinion, in my point of view.

À noite, todos os gatos são pardos. – All cats are gray during the dark.

À pala. – For free.

A pensar morreu um burro. – When somebody takes too long to make an easy decision, overthinking it.

A pensar na morte da bezerra. – To mope around.

A verdade é como o azeite, vem sempre ao de cima. – Truth, like oil, will in time rise to the surface.

Água mole em pedra dura, tanto bate até que fura. – Water dropping day by day wears the hardest rock away.

Aguenta os cavalos! – Hold your horses!

Amigos amigos, negócios à parte. – Friends friends, business aside.

Andar à nora. – When someone is not aware

Ao sabor da mare/vento! – To go with the flow.

Aqui há gato. – When somebody is sensing something is going on.

Armar um 31! – To create a chaotic situation, a fight, or a big problem.

Barata tonta! – A kind of aloof person that is confused and sloppy.

Burro velho não aprende línguas. – You can't teach an old dog new tricks.

Cão que ladra não morde. – Barking dogs never bite.

Cu de Judas. – In the middle of nowhere.

De boas intenções está o inferno cheio. – The road to hell is paved with good intentions.

Diz-me com quem andas e dir-te-ei quem és. – He who sleeps with dogs, gets up with fleas.

Em terra de cego, quem tem um olho é rei. – In the land of the blind, the one-eyed man is king.

Entre marido e mulher, não se mete a colher. – It means that no one should meddle in a couple's affairs or quarrels.

Estou com os azeites. – When somebody is in a bad mood.

Faço isto com uma perna às costas. – I can do this with my hands tied/in my sleep.

Fazer asneira. – Screw up.

Fazer de vela. – Being the third wheel.

Mais vai prevenir que remediar. – An ounce of prevention is worth a pound of cure.

Melhor tarde que nunca. – Better late than never.

Não adianta chorar sobre leite derramado. – It's no use crying over spilled milk.

Não é grande espingarda. – When something is not very good.

Não faço ideia. – I haven't got a clue.

Nem que a vaca tussa. – Not in a million years.

O gato comeu-lhe a língua. – When somebody doesn't say anything at all.

O pior cego é aquele que não quer ver. – There is no worse blind man than the one who doesn't want to see.

Por uma unha negra/por um triz. – By the skin of our teeth.

Pulga atrás da orelha. – When something is suspicious.

Quem anda à chuva molha-se. – It means that when you put yourself in certain situations, you'll have to deal with its consequences.

Quem me dera! – I wish!

Quem não arrisca, não petisca. – No pain, no gain.

Quem ri por último, ri melhor. – He who laughs last, laughs best.

Quem sai aos seus não degenera. – The apple doesn't fall far from the tree.

Só por cima do meu cadáver. – Over my dead body!

Tenho um olho no burro, o outro no cigano. –   Paying attention to everything that is going on around you.

Verdade nua e crua. – The whole, unvarnished truth.

Slang terms

We have decided to include a list of slang terms in this book as they are a big component of a language, especially for whoever wants to be fluent, to learn it fully and properly, and to then use it with natives. Additionally, it is something that is not usually thought of when teaching the language to foreigners, but it is something that is a part of the language, undoubtedly. And if the natives when they're young are exposed to all of the slang, foreigners are learning the language from a book or in a classroom, where formal speech is encouraged, and slang is often not appropriated at all. However, it would be impossible to understand the Portuguese spoken in Portugal in an every-day situation if you don't know the basic slang terms, which people use all the time, even at a café or restaurant. Plus, if you're starting a conversation with somebody new, it will always be a good thing to add some slang to your vocabulary—that will impress them for sure! À borla – For free

À toa – Someone doing something without putting much thought into it

Abananado – Shaken, confused

Abancar – To sit down

Afiambrar – Get close or hold of something that likely you were not supposed to.

Arrochar – Fall asleep

Até sabe a pato – Something that is really appreciated

Bacano – A cool dude

Banhada – To steal or to fool someone

Baril – Cool, nice

Bater a bota – Die

Bater couro – To woe, hit on someone

Beca – A little

Beijoca – Little kiss

Bezana – Being wasted

Bica – Expresso

Bimbo – A fool, hillbilly

Bué – A lot

Cadela – Being wasted

Cagar – Poo

Carcanhol – Money

Chavalo – Dude

Cochilo – Nap

Coiso/a – Thingy

Cortes – To bail out of something

Curtir – Make out with someone, or enjoy something

Dar bandeira – Draw attention

Dar barra – To deny something to someone, quite unexpectedly

Dar cana – Draw attention

Esticar o pernil – Die

Fino – Tap beer

Fixe – Cool, nice

Fogo! – Damn!

Ganda mel – Very nice, good

Gato/a – Hot dude or girl

Gregar – Vomit

Guita – Money

Jajão – Fail

Mão de vaca – Cheap person

Massa – Money

Meu – Dude, man

Mijar – Pee

Molhe – A lot

Na boa – It's cool

Narsa – Drunk, wasted

Nite – Cigarette

Papel – Money

Pasta – Money

Pilim – Money

Poça! – Damn!

Porrada – Beating

Puxa! – Yikes!

Tá-se bem – That's okay

Tipo – Like (something)

Tótil – A lot

Tranqui – Relax (short for "Tranquilo")

Um coche – A bit

Xoné – A fool, crazy person

Xôxo – Peck on the cheek

Ya – Yes

Pocket dictionary

We have prepared this small dictionary for you so that whenever you're in need of finding the translation or the correct spelling for a word you don't know or remember, you have the answer close by. This will obviously help you throughout the reading of this book, but also after you're done with it—if you ever feel you have to brush up on your vocabulary or just make sure the word you're looking for is the right one, this pocket dictionary will be a great tool. If, in any case, the word you are looking for is not in our dictionary, check out this high-quality and reliable online dictionary - **Cambridge Dictionary**.

A billion – Um bilião

A million – Um milhão

A thousand – Mil

Accelerator – Acelerador

Accident – Acidente

Achilles tendon – Tendão de Aquiles

Adam's apple – Maçã-de-adão

Agnostic – Agnótico

Alcoholic – Alcóolico

Anatomy – Anatomia

Anchovy – Anchova

Animals – Animais

Ankle – Tornozelo

Annual – Anual

Ant – Formiga

Anus – Ânus

Appendix – Apêndice

Apple – Maçã

Apple Tree – Macieira

April – Abril

April Fools – Dia das Mentiras

Arm – Braço

Armpit – Axila/Sovaco

Artery – Artéria

Atheist – Ateu/ateia

August – Agosto

Aunt – Tia

Automatic – Automático

Baby foods – Comida de bebé

Baby wipes – Toalhitas de bebé

Back – Costas

Back seat – Lugar de trás

Backbone – Coluna vertebral

Bag – Saco

Bagpack – Mochila

Balance – Saldo

Barley - Cevada

Batteries – Pilhas

Battery – Bateria

Bear – Urso

Beard – Barba

Bee – Abelha

Beef – Vaca

Beer – Cerveja

Belly – Barriga

Belly button – Umbigo

Belt – Cinto

Best friend – Melhor amigo/a

Beverages – Bebidas

Bicycle – Bicicleta

Big toe – Dedo grande

Bile – Bílis

Bird – Pássaro

Black – Preto

Bladder – Bexiga

Blinker – Piscas

Blood – Sangue

Blossom – Florescer

Blouse – Blusa

Blue – Azul

Boat – Barco

Bone – Osso

Books – Livros

Bottle – Garrafa

Bottom – Rabo

Bowl – Tigela

Boy – Rapaz/Menino

Boyfriend – Namorado

Brain – Cérebro

Brake light – Luz de travão

Branch – Ramo

Brassiere – Soutien

Bread counter – Padaria

Breasts – Seios

Breath – Hálito

Breathing – Respiração

Breeze – Brisa

Brother-in-law – Cunhado

Brown – Castanho

Buddhist – Budista

Bug – Bicho / Insecto

Bull – Touro

Bumper – Autocolante

Bush – Arbusto

Butter – Manteiga

Butterfly – Borboleta

Buttocks – Nádegas

Cable – Cabo

Cactus – Cacto

Calf (body part) – Gémeo

Camping – Acampar

Cancel – Cancelar

Candle – Vela

Car – Carro

Caravan – Caravana

Card – Cartão

Carnival – Carnaval

Cartilage – Cartilagem

Cat – Gato

Catholic – Católico

Century – Século

Cheap – Barato

Cheek – Bochecha

Cheese – Queijo

Cherry – Cereja

Cherry tree – Cerejeira

Chest – Peito

Chestnut tree – Castanheiro

Chicken – Galinha/Frango

Child – Criança

Child Seat – Cadeira de criança

Chin – Queixo

Chocolate – Chocolate

Christian – Cristão

Christmas – Natal

Christmas Eve – Consoada

Church – Igreja

Cider – Sidra

Clams – Amêijoas

Claw – Garra

Climate – Clima

Clock – Relógio

Clouds – Nuvens

Clutch – Embraiagem

Cock – Galo

Coconut - Coco

Codfish – Bacalhau

Coffee – Café

Cold – Frio

Collarbone/clavicle – Clavícula

Cologne – Colónia

Colors – Cores

Components - Componentes

Conditioner – Amaciador

Condoms – Preservativos

Convertible – Descapotável

Corn – Milho

Cornea – Córnea

Cotton – Algodão

Country – País

Cousin – Primo/a

Cow – Vaca

Crab – Caranguejo

Crow – Corvo

Cry – Choro

Cup – Chávena

Cutlery – Talheres

Cyclist – Ciclista

Dashboard – Tablier

Daughter – Filha

Daughter-in-law – Nora

Day after tomorrow – Depois de amanhã

Day before yesterday – Anteontem

Day off – Folga

Days of the week – Dias da semana

December – Dezembro

Deer – Veado

Defecate – Defecar

Degrees – Graus

Dental floss – Fio dental

Deodorant – Desodorizante

Desserts – Sobremesas

Diapers – Fraldas

Diesel – Gasóleo

Dog – cão

Door lock – Fechadura da porta

Dove – Pomba

Dress – Vestido

Drinks – Bebidas

Drive – Conduzir

Driver's seat – Lugar do condutor

Drought – Seca

Dry – Seco

Duck – Pato

Eagle – Águia

Ear – Orelha/Ouvido

Eardrum – Tímpano

Earlobe – Lóbulo da orelha

Easter – Páscoa

Egg – Ovo

Eight – Oito

Eight hundred – Oitocentos

Eighteen – Dezoito

Eighty – Oitenta

Elbow – Cotovelo

Elephant – Elefante

Eleven – Onze

Emergency – Emergência

Envelopes – Envelopes

Evacuate – Evacuar

Exhaust – Exaustor

Expensive – Caro

Eye – Olho

Eyeball – Globo ocular

Eyebrow – Sobrancelha

Eyelash – Pestana

Eyelid – Pálpebra

Face Powder – Pó de arroz

Fall – Outono

Family – Família

Fashion – Moda

Fat – Gordura

Father-in-law – Sogro

February – Fevereiro

Fiancé/e – Noivo/a

Fifteen – Quinze

Fifty – Cinquenta

Fig tree – Figueira

Finger – Dedos

Fingernail – Unha

Fire – Fogo

Firewood – Lenha

First aid kit – Kit primeiros Socorros

Fish – Peixe

Five – Cinco

Five hundred – Quinhentos

Flashlight – Lanterna

Flat tire – Pneu furado

Flesh – Carne

Flower – Flor

Fly – Mosca

Flies – Moscas

Fog – Nevoeiro

Food – Comida

Foot – Pé

Forearm – Antebraço

Forecast – Previsão

Forehead – Testa

Fork – Garfo

Forty – Quarenta

Foundation – Base

Four – Quarto

Four hundred – Quatrocentos

Fourteen – Catorze

Fox – Raposa

Freckles – Sardas

Freezing – Gelado

Friday – Sexta-feira

Friend – Amigo/a

Frog – Sapo

Front seat – Lugar da frente

Fruit tree – Árvore de fruto

Fruits – Frutas

Fuel – Combustível

Fuel tank – Depósito de combustível

Full – Cheio/a

Full beam lights – Máximos

Fur – Pêlo

Fuse – Fusível

Garage – Garage

Garlic – Alho

Gas – Gasolina/Gás

Gas pedal – Acelerador

Gentleman – Cavalheiro

Giraffe – Girafa

Girl – Rapariga/Menina

Girlfriend – Namorada

Gland – Glândula

Glass – Vidro/Copo

Glove compartment – Porta-luvas

Gloves – Luvas

Glue – Cola

Goat – Cabra

God – Deus

Goddaughter – Afilhada

Godfather – Padrinho

Godmother – Madrinha

Godson – Aflhado

Granddaughter – Neta

Grandfather – Avô

Grandmother – Avó

Grandparents – Avós

Grandson – Neto

Grapes – Uvas

Grass – Relva

Gray – Cinzento

Green – Verde

Groin – Virilha

Hair – Cabelo

Hairbrush – Escova de cabelo

Hairspray – Laca

Hake – Pescada

Halloween – Dia das Bruxas

Ham – Fiambre

Hand – Mão

Handbrake – Travão

Handkerchiefs – Lenços

Hat – Chapéu

Head – Cabeça

Headlights – Faróis

Headphones – Auscultadores

Headrest – Encosto

Hearing/sound – Audição

Heart – Coração

Heat – Calor

Heel – Calcanhar

Help – Ajuda/Socorro

Herb – Erva

Hiccup – Soluço

High – Alto/a

High heels – Sapatos Altos

Hip – Anca

Holiday – Feriado

Hoof – Casco

Horn – Buzina

Horse – Cavalo

Horse mackerel – Carapau

Hot – Quente

Humidity – Humidade

Hurricane - Furacão

Husband – Marido

Ice – Gelo

Ignition – Ignição

Indicators – Indicadores

Insurance – Seguro

Intestines – Intestino

Iris – Íris

Jack – Macaco

Jacket – Casaco

Jam – Compota

January – Janeiro

Jaw – Maxilar

Jelly – Gelatina

Jewish – Judeu

Joints – Articulações

Juice – Sumo

July – Julho

June – Junho

Kidneys – Rins

Knee – Joelho

Kneecap – Rótula

Knife – Faca

Knuckles – Nós dos dedos

Kyte – Papagaio

Lamb – Cordeiro

Lamp – Lamparina

Large intestine – Intestino grosso

Laxatives – Laxantes

Leaf – Folha

Leap year – Ano bissexto

Leather – Couro

Left – Esquerda

Leg – Perna

Lemon – Limão

Lemonade – Limonada

Light bulb – Lâmpada

Lighter – Isqueiro

Lightning – Trovões

Limb – Membro

Lime – Lima

Lion - Leão

Lip – Lábio

Lipstick – Baton

Liver – Fígado

Locker – Cadeado

Lost – Perdido/a

Low – Baixo/a

Lungs – Pulmões

Magazines – Revistas

Man – Homem

Manager – Gestor

March – Março

Mascara – Rímel

Matches – Fósforos

May – Maio

Meat – Carne

Meat section – Talho

Mechanic – Mecânico

Menstruation – Menstruação

Meteorology – Metereologia

Milk – Leite

Milkshake – Batido

Minibus - Miniautocarro

Mirror – Espelho

Moisturizing cream – Creme hidratante

Monday – Segunda-feira

Monkey – Macaco

Monthly – Mensal

Months – Meses

Moon – Lua

Moonlight – Luar

Mosque – Mesquita

Mosquitoes – Mosquitos

Moss – Musgo

Mother-in-law – Sogra

Motor – Motor

Motorbike – Motocicleta

Mountains – Montanhas

Mouse – Rato

Mustache – Bigode

Mouth – Boca

Mouthwash – Elixir Bocal

Mr. – Senhor

Mrs. – Senhora

Mucus – Muco

Muscle – Músculo

Mushroom – Cogumelo

Nail scissors – Corta-unhas

Napkin – Guardanapo

Neck – Pescoço

Needle – Agulha

Nephew – Sobrinho

Nerve – Nervo

Nervous system – Sistema nervoso

New Year's Eve – Véspera de Ano Novo

Newspaper – Jornal

Niece – Sobrinha

Nine – Nove

Nine hundred – Novecentos

Nineteen – Dezanove

Ninety – Noventa

Nipple – Mamilo

Nose – Nariz

Nostril – Narina

November – Novembro

Number plate – Matrícula

Numbers - Números

Nuts – Frutos Secos

Oat – Aveia

October – Outubro

Oesophagus – Esófago

Oil – Óleo

Ointment/pomade – Pomada

Olive oil – Azeite

Olive tree – Oliveira

Olives – Azeitonas

One – Um[16]

One hundred – Cem[17]16

Onion – Cebola

Orange – Cor-de-laranja

Orange – Laranja

Organ – Orgão

Outdoor – Exterior

Owl – Coruja

Painkillers – Analgésicos

Palm – Palma

Palm tree – Palmeira

Pancreas – Pâncreas

Pants – Calças

Paper – Papel

Passenger seat – Lugar do passageiro/pendura

Paw – Pata

Peanut butter – Manteiga de Amendoim

Peanuts – Amendoins

---

[16] Numbers one and two also have a feminine form when written before feminine nouns. So, "One boy – *um* menino" / "one girl – *uma* menina" and "Two boys – *dois* meninos / two girls – *duas* meninas".

[17] Every number over a hundred follows that same rule of the numbers over 20, but instead of saying "*cem* e um", it's said "*cento* e um", *cento* e dois", and so on.

Pear – Pêra

Pear tree – Pereira

Pee – Fazer xixi

Pelvis – Pélvis

Pen – Caneta

Pencil – Lápis

Pepper – Pimenta

Perfume – Perfume

Period – Período

Petal – Pétala

Phone charger – Carregador de Telemóvel

Photographs – Fotografias

Pig – Porco

Pigeon – Pombo

Pine tree - Pinheiro

Pineapple – Ananás

Pink – Cor-de-rosa

Piston – Pistão

Plants – Plantas

Plate – Prato

Plum tree – Pessegueiro

Pollen – Pólen

Poo – Fazer cocó

Pork – Porco

Pot – Panela

Pregnant – Grávida

Prescription – Prescrição

Pressure – Pressão

Protestant – Protestante

Pupil – Pupila

Purple – Roxo

Quit – Sair

Rabbit – Coelho

Radiator – Radiador

Rain – Chuva

Rainbow – Arco-íris

Rat - Ratazana

Rattlesnake – Cascavel

Razor – Lâmina/gillette

Razor clam – Lingueirão

Rear windscreen – Pára-brisas traseiro

Rearview mirror – Espelho retrovisor

Rectum – Recto

Red – Vermelho

Region – Região

Religion – Religião

Retina – Retina

Rib – Costela

Rib cage – Caixa Torácica

Right - Left

Road – Estrada

Roof – Tecto

Root – Raiz

Rope – Corda

Rose – Rosa

Safety pin – Pin de segurança

Saliva/spit – Saliva/cuspe

Salmon – Salmão

Salt – Sal

Sangria – Sangria

Sanitary pad – Penso higiénico

Sanitary towels – Toalhitas higiénicas

Sardine – Sardinha

Saturday – Sábado

Sausage – Salsicha

Scarf – Lenço

Scissors – Tesouras

Scooter – Scooter

Sea bass – Robalo

Sea bream – Dourada

Seahorse – Cavalo-marinho

Seasons – Estações

Seat belt – Cinto de segurança

Semen – Sémen

Semester – Semestre

Senses – Sentidos

September – Setembro

Serpent – Serpente

Serum – Soro

Seven – Sete

Seven hundred – Setecentos

Seventeen – Dezassete

Seventy – Setenta

Shampoo – Champô

Shark – Tubarão

Shaving cream – Creme de barbear

Shaving foam – Espuma de barbear

Shaving gel – Gel de barbear

Sheep – Ovelha

Shellfish – Marisco

Shin – Canela

Shock absorber – Pára-choques

Shoes – Sapatos / Calçado

Shorts – Calções

Shoulder – Ombro

Sight – Visão

Sister-in-law – Cunhada

Six – Seis

Six hundred – Seiscentos

Sixteen – Dezasseis

Sixty – Sessenta

Skeleton – Esqueleto

Skin – Pele

Skirt – Saia

Skull – Crânio

Sky – Céu

Skylight – Clarabóia

Sleeping bag – Saco-cama

Small intestine – Intestino delgado

Smell – Olfacto

Snake – Cobra

Sneakers – Sapatilhas / Ténis

Sneeze – Espirro

Snow – Neve

Snow tires – Pneus para a neve

Soap – Sabão

Socks – Meias

Soda – Refrigerante

Sole – Planta

Son – Filho

Son-in-law – Genro

Sour – Azedo

Souvenirs – Lembranças

Spare tire – Pneu sobresselente

Speedometer – Velocímetro

Spicy – Picante

Spider – Aranha

Spine – Espinha

Spleen – Baço

Spoon – Colher

Spring – Primavera

State – Estado

Steering wheel – Volante

Stepdaughter – Enteada

Stepfather – Padrasto

Stepmother – Madrasta

Stepson – Enteado

Stomach – Estômago

Storm – Tempestade

Strawberries – Morango

Straws – Palhinhas

Suit – Fato

Summer – Verão

Sun lotion – Protector solar

Sunday – Domingo

Sunglasses – Óculos de Sol

Sunny – Solarengo

Sweat – Suor

Sweet – Doce

Swimsuit – Fato de banho

Synagogue – Sinagoga

Table towel – Toalha de mesa

Tail – Cauda

Tampons – Tampões

Taste – Palato/paladar

Taxi – Táxi

Tea – Chá

Tears – Lágrimas

Teeth – Dentes

Temperature – Temperatura

Temple – Templo

Ten – Dez

Tendon – Tendão

Tent – Tenda

Testicles – Testículos

Thermometer – Termómetro

Thigh – Coxa

Thigh bone/femur – Fémur

Thirteen – Treze

Thirty – Trinta

Thorn – Espinho

Thousand – Mil

Three – Três

Three hundred – Trezentos

Throat – Garganta

Thumb – Polegar

Thunder – Trovoada

Thursday – Quinta-feira

Ticket office – Bilheteira

Tiger – Tigre

Tire – Pneu

Tissues – Lenços

Toe – Dedo do pé

Toenail – Unha do pé

Toilet paper – Papel higiénico

Tomorrow – Amanhã

Tongue – Língua

Tooth – Dente

Toothbrush – Escova de dentes

Toothpaste – Pasta de dentes

Tornado – Tornado

Touch – Tacto

Town – Cidade

Tractor – Tractor

Trailer – Atrelado

Tram – Elétrico

Tree – Árvore

Trimester – Trimestre

Trout – Truta

Truck – Camião

Trunk (car) – Bagageira

Trunk (elephant's) – Tromba

Trunk (tree) – Tronco

Tuesday – Terça-feira

Tuna – Atum

Turkey – Peru

Turquoise – Turquesa

Tweezers – Pinças

Twelve – Doze

Twenty – Vinte[18]

Twig – Galho

Two – Dois

Two hundred – Duzentos

Umbrella – Chapéu de chuva

Uncle – Tio

Underpants – Cuecas

Underwear – Roupa interior

Unleaded gas – Gasolina sem chumbo

Urgent – Urgente

Urinate – Urinar

Urine – Urina

Utensils – Utensílios

---

[18] After 20, every number in between 20 and 99, excluding 30, 40, 50, 60, 70, 80, 90 is the number itself plus and one, or and two, etc. So 21 would be "vinte *e um*", 31 would be "trinta *e dois»*", and so on.

Vagina – Vagina

Valentine's Day – Dia dos Namorados

Valve – Válvula

Van – Carrinha

Vegetables – Vegetais

Vein – Veia

Vertebra – Vértebra

View – Vista

Vinegar – Vinagre

Vitamin pills – Vitamínicos

Vomit – Vómito

Waist – Cintura

Warning light – Luz de aviso

Wasp – Vespa

Watch – Relógio

Water – Água

Wave – Onda

Weather – Tempo

Wednesday – Quarta-feira

Weekly – Semanal

Wheat – Trigo

Whelk – Búzios

Wife – Esposa

Wind – Vento

Window – Janela

Windpipe – Traqueia

Windscreen – Pára-brisas

Wine – Vinho

Wing – Asa

Winter – Inverno

Wolf – Lobo

Woman – Mulher

Womb – Útero

Wrinkles – Rugas

Wrist – Pulso

Wristwatch – Relógio de pulso

Yawn – Bocejar

Yellow – Amarelo

Yesterday – Ontem

Zero – Zero

Conclusion

Portuguese: How to Learn Portuguese Fast, Including Grammar, Short Stories, and Useful Phrases is aimed to give a basic understanding of the Portuguese language to beginners by laying out the fundamental grammar rules and overall structure of the language. However, its intent was not only to aid those who are just starting out on their trip into the rich world of the Portuguese language but also to continue guiding those who have already established and built a solid knowledge of the idiom. Having adopted both a non-communicative and a semi-communicative teaching method, this book first set out to give the basic tools needed to understand and speak the language. After that, a storytelling approach presented the reader with real-life situations and events, where they were encouraged to engage with the story, characters, and narrative, thus reducing the chances of demotivation, loss of interest, or boredom. Hopefully, this book served its purpose and was captivating enough to make you fall in love with the Portuguese language. It was paramount to offer a pleasant and exciting learning experience, which ultimately resulted in you being able to understand and express yourself in Portuguese.

Lastly—and this cannot be stressed enough—keep practicing your Portuguese! Learning a language requires a lot of studying and hard work. So do not throw away all the hours that you have spent taking these first steps. It is recommended that you revisit this book whenever you feel like you have to brush up on your vocabulary or grammar. Do not forget that as you advance to more demanding linguistic challenges, the knowledge learned here, as basic as it may appear, at first sight, is absolutely crucial when it comes to mastering the Portuguese language. Here is some final advice on what you can do to practice your skills:

- Read books! Either other learning books, or novels (always with your dictionary at hand);

- Practice your writing skills – try to write your shopping list in Portuguese, for example;

- Watch Portuguese movies – with subtitles in your original language, and as you develop your skills, with Portuguese subtitles;

- Hear music – check out the lyrics, and search for the words you are not familiar with and sing! (Music will also help with the correct pronunciation and accent);

- Visit Portuguese-speaking countries – there is no better way to learn than being completely immersed in the language, surrounded by real-life situations, and interacting with natives.

Certainly, your tenacity and perseverance will be rewarded at the end.